Stamford Bridge Legends
Chelsea
Champions

Stamford Bridge Legends
Chelsea Champions

Author David Lane

Published by
Legends Publishing
22 Park Road
Hampton Hill
Middlesex
TW12 1HF

E-mail info@legendspublishing.net
Website www.legendspublishing.net

Copyright 2003 by Legends Publishing

ISBN: 0-9543682-3-1

First Edition

Printed and bound in the United Kingdom

Foreword
& Contents

Over the past six months I have written and produced this unique book in co-operation with a very special band of 'Chelsea Pensioners' - the Championship squad of 1955. With Chelsea Football Club's centenary coinciding with the fiftieth anniversary of their only top flight title crown, Legends Publishing and the players thought it was the perfect time to relive their amazing achievements, and in doing so, hopefully raise some funds to help these Chelsea heroes in their later years. The players themselves will earn a healthy slice of any profits this book makes.

I hope you agree that their stories make fascinating reading - you'll be taken back to an era in stark contrast to today's and learn what it was really like to clinch the Championship, not through the interpretations of a researcher or historian, but through the words of the men who fought for glory out there on the pitch, the players themselves.

Roman Abramovic's dramatic arrival has without doubt energised Chelsea like never before, but in doing so, has further raised expectations among Blues fans and the media. It will therefore be interesting to see how events unfold over the next few seasons and whether history will repeat itself in the most coincidental way imaginable - will Chelsea win the Premiership in their Centenary just as they did the First Division in their Golden Jubilee season? Or won't club die-hards have to wait that long?

Quite what the future holds can't be known right now, so while Blues fans await a second team of top flight title winners, join the 1954-55 players in a nostalgic celebration and relive the personal and heartfelt memories of Chelsea Football Club's true Champions!

David Lane

Thanks to - The 1955 Chelsea squad, Albert Sewell, Katie Cheeseman, Martin Holland, Greville Waterman, Rita Lane, Jen Little [Empics] and Colorsport.

Photographs - Every effort has been made to trace the copyright holders of the photographs used in this book, however, the majority of the pictures came from the player's personal collections and had no information attached.

How The Title Was Won

From
Chelsea Champions 1955

To have followed Chelsea closely during their first three seasons under Ted Drake was to have seen tradition halted and shaped anew. Down the years the club had gained notoriety for its great names and artistic football with the emphasis on individual performance, and an exasperating lack of achievement.

All that changed. Ted Drake gave Stamford Bridge a new heart and Chelsea's football a streamlined look. The team-sheet listed no star outshining everyone around him, punch displaced frills and decoration in the style of play, and through the club ran a spirit such had never been seen before.

And in a story-book climax to the fifty-year pageant, Chelsea won the Football League Championship in 1955, their year of Golden Jubilee. What exquisite timing! I would agree at once with those that said in previous years the Championship had gone to far greater *footballing* sides than the Chelsea line-up of 1954-55, but hastily add the belief that none surpassed the Chelsea Champions in their magnificently spirited approach to every match throughout the season.

No club had tried longer or harder for their first major honour, and Chelsea's ultimate success served as an inspiration to all in sport who strove year in year out for rewards that never seemed to come. The popularity of Chelsea's triumph could be gauged by the fact that over a thousand telegrams and letters of congratulation were received at Stamford Bridge. The turnstiles also told a tale - home attendances for League matches exceeded a million for the first time, and the average gate of 48,350 was the highest in the country.

Most of the credit for what was accomplished went, of course, to Ted Drake, but he preferred to praise his board of directors and staff for the maximum support they gave in developing the new Chelsea.

The Drake plan was to comb the Third Division for potential First Division players and blend them with the best talent he inherited at Stamford Bridge. In carrying it out he did not escape criticism. 'You cannot build a First Division side with Third Division footballers,' was the cry from those clamouring for immediate success. Drake was not dismayed. In time he proved his detractors wrong. How well he had duplicated certain positions was revealed during the Championship season.

Two players appeared in every match - Derek Saunders and Eric Parsons. At left-half Saunders, ex-Walthamstow and England amateur international, made his mark as one of the most improved players of the year. His tackling, always full of weight, was little short of severe and allied to it were sound anticipation plus good distribution skills. Parsons was Chelsea's will-o'-the-wisp. He wore the number seven shirt, but nimble feet carried him to every forward position and most defen-

February 1955 – Ted Drake looks on from the dug-out

sive ones as well, sometimes to the embarrassment of the men behind. How the crowds thrilled to his crouching, top-speed runs; the more they roared the better did this human dynamo respond.

In goal, Bill Robertson, with the massive hands, appeared regularly until the end of January when he damaged an ankle in training. Charlie Thompson, a fellow Scot, deputised so well that Robertson spent the rest of the season with the reserves.

At full-back the situation arose in which John Harris, Peter Sillett and Stan Willemse vied for two positions. Harris and Willemse formed the early combination, but once Sillett had established himself as captain of the England Under-23 team and as a sure-shot penalty-kicker, a permanent place had to be found for him, to the ultimate exclusion of Harris. The years rested lightly on Harris. He played in three-quarters of the season's programme and richly deserved his Championship medal, considering the wonderful service he had given the club, mostly through difficult days.

Sillett, of the giant build and deceptively casual approach, was only twenty-one and with one swing of his powerful boot could transfer play from one end to the other, and none of his contemporaries in the game today hit the dead ball with greater velocity. *Continued on page 11*

When Ted took over at Stamford Bridge in May 1952, he ventured: "Perhaps we shall be ready for honours in three years' time." He delivered right on schedule, winning the League Championship in 1955, which caused a swift change of title to the club's first official history from 'Chelsea Jubilee' (commemorating their fiftieth year) to 'Chelsea Champions.

But he was not immediately popular with the fans. One of Drake's first decisions was to drop the legendary Pensioner as the club's trademark, awarding him a "permanent and well-earned rest."

I was privileged to write Ted's programme notes with him through the nine years he was at Stamford Bridge. He remains unique in the club's history as still the only manager to win the League Championship for Chelsea. It took fifty years to reach that milestone. Are they going to wait until their centenary in 2005 to win it again?

Albert Sewell

Willemse's very presence added tremendous gusto to the side. There remained a few untidy edges to his play that were unlikely to be smoothed over at that stage of his career, but he was a lion at heart, a battler for ninety minutes of every match, and was an inspiration on many occasions that led to the Championship crown.

Like Harris, right-half Ken Armstrong had gone beyond the three hundred appearances mark in First Division games for Chelsea, and everyone at Stamford Bridge was delighted to see him win his first cap for England against Scotland at Wembley in April 1955. Nowhere in the game would you find a better example of the true club man.

Between Armstrong and Saunders stood the towering figure of Stan Wicks at centre-half. He succeeded Ron Greenwood in mid-season, and grew more dominating each week as the Championship assault mounted. Goalkeeper Charlie Thomson paid handsome tribute to him when he said at the time: 'Stan makes a goalkeeper's job simple. He gets practically every ball in the air and doesn't miss many tricks on the ground.'

Parsons' right-wing partner, Johnny McNichol, was the typical Scottish-style ball-player. He did his best work at close quarters, and although at times he overplayed the short game he did a thorough job in keeping Parsons well supplied and also found the opportunity to score fourteen goals himself.

The distinction of leading Chelsea to their first Championship went to Roy Bentley, another who had seen the club through past storms. When Chelsea went to the top of the League by winning at Cardiff on 23rd March 1955, Roy promised Chairman Joe Mears 'We're there for the rest of the season.' And although he did not score again until the very last match, he kept the line moving well enough for the promise to be fulfilled. Bentley's record for the season was twenty-one goals in forty-one matches. He scored two hat-tricks, one for England against Wales at Wembley, the other for Chelsea against Newcastle.

The original left-wing selection was Leslie Stubbs and Frank Blunstone, but two amateurs also played a part. While injury kept Blunstone out for the early months, Jim Lewis stepped in, and later came Seamus O'Connell, the Bishop Auckland and England amateur, as challenger for the inside-left position. Stubbs had to work hard for his reward - five goals in twenty-seven games - whereas O'Connell played only ten matches yet scored seven times. O'Connell could always be singled out on his travels between London and the North - he carried the tools of his trade, his boots, unwrapped and dangling by the laces.

At outside-left Blunstone added youth and subtle ball-play to the attack. The twenty-year-old son of a Crewe railwayman with seven brothers and five sisters, Blunstone seemed to thrive on the demands of combining Chelsea with National Service Army unit football and made the first of five England appearances against Wales at Wembley in November 1954. At the end of the season he had played more than a hundred matches! Not surprisingly he was feeling the effects of so much continuous football.

Only twice since the First Division was enlarged to twenty-two clubs in 1919 had the Championship been won with as few points as fifty-two. The previous occasions were in 1929 by Sheffield Wednesday and 1939 by Arsenal. Both those clubs had got there by a single point; Chelsea, in 1955, finished four ahead of the runners-up, Wolves.

They certainly promised much right from the start - two wins and three draws equalled their longest unbeaten opening to a season (three wins and two draws in 1922), but, hardened by years of disappointment, the fans were not going to be swept off their feet at that.

Best of the early results was a three-one win at Newcastle on 25th September. Chelsea had recorded only one previous League victory at St. James' Park (in 1909, also by three-one), and this performance placed them fourth from top compared with second from bottom on the corresponding Saturday twelve months previously.

October brought the Blues down to earth with a bump - one point from five matches and a fall to twelfth in the table. Yet two of those games bristled with excitement. West Bromwich Albion, Cup-holders and League leaders, arrived at Stamford Bridge on 2nd October with a boast of fifteen points from their last eight matches. The gates having been closed at 67,440, Roy Bentley quickly earned a roar of appreciation for his hundredth League goal for the club. Ten minutes from time Chelsea led three-one and were ready to go top of the First Division, but Albion ruined that prospect by scoring twice, their equaliser two minutes from time shot at long range by left-back and Captain Millard, who otherwise had a nightmare game against Parsons.

A fortnight later fans witnessed possibly the most action packed game ever seen at Stamford Bridge, though this time the gate was reduced to 56,000 because of a bus strike. A match of superb forward play resulted Chelsea five, Manchester United six. Quite a day for Seamus O'Connell to make his debut! And quite a debut, with three O'Connell goals in a riot of scoring that went 0-1, 1-1, 2-1, 2-2, 2-3 (half-time), 2-4, 2-5, 3-5, 3-6, 4-6, 5-6. Eight of those goals were condensed into thirty-two minutes, and the crowd were in a frenzy as Chelsea worked off the arrears. How the Manchester United side held out during the last twelve pulsating minutes nobody knew. One more goal in the visitors' net and this fantastic match would have equalled the League record for a drawn match - Leicester City six, Arsenal six in April 1930. So, for the moment,

October 1954 — Action from the Chelsea-Manchester United goal-feast

United went top of the table after an absolute epic, the finest game seen for years at Stamford Bridge but, ironically, one that provided no points towards Chelsea's Championship.

A first chance for Stan Wicks and the return of Frank Blunstone at Sunderland on 6th November coincided with Chelsea's return to point-winning ways after four one-goal defeats. They drew three-all, and Blunstone played himself into the England team meeting Wales at Wembley four days later for his first cap. From inside-right in the same attack Roy Bentley scored all his country's goals in a three-two win - the first England hat-trick for five seasons.

November yielded two home wins (Tottenham and Portsmouth) and two away draws (Sunderland and Sheffield Wednesday), including the first victory at Stamford Bridge for eleven weeks, and the opening match in December gave substance to the Championship hopes. Chelsea visited Molineux, where Wolverhampton had crushed them eight-one the year before, and this time brought home the points by four goals to three after a magnificent finish to a classic in the mud. With ten minutes left Chelsea led two-one. Then Wolves levelled and almost at once Hancocks put them three-two ahead from a hotly disputed penalty. That might have been the end for other teams, or the Chelsea of other

December 1954 — Red Banner's goalie, Olah, catches during the 2-2 draw

years, but this Chelsea went furiously for goal. Stubbs made it three-all in the eighty-fourth minute and seconds later Bentley lashed in the winner. Man of the match in Chelsea's first success at Molineux for eighteen years was Parsons. He revelled in the mud, repeatedly plough-ing his way through and leaving opponents at a standstill.

Next came a four-nil win against Aston Villa, followed on Wednesday, 15th December, by the challenge of Red Banner, the crack Hungarian club with almost a full team of Internationals. Never was there such a wide gulf between expectation and realisation. Neither side showed anything like proper form, ill feeling interfered with the play and everyone was relieved to hear the final whistle with the score two-all. Hidegkuti scored first for the Hungarians, Stubbs and Bentley scrambled goals for Chelsea before half-time and Palotas equalised twenty minutes from the end. To the cartoonists' delight and the disbelief of a 40,000 crowd, three penalty-kicks were missed in a blistering spell between the fortieth and fifty-second minutes. John Harris began the fantasy by shooting wide from the spot after a handling offence. Then Lantos did likewise after Harris handled. Three minutes later Willemse bulldozed his way past four opponents from the centre of the field and was upended when about to shoot from an odds-on scoring position. Reluctantly, but dutifully, Harris again took the penalty; again he aimed to the right and, to an accompanying gasp all round the ground, saw Olah smother the ball on the goal-line.

Having now missed three penalties in a row (the other was against Spurs the previous month), Harris stood down from the job in the next match, against Leicester City. A penalty duly arrived, and on this occasion Bentley misfired, Anderson turning his shot behind. It did not prevent Chelsea winning three-one, and their second goal was one of the strangest on record. McNichol shot against the crossbar and the ball rebounded between two Leicester men, Froggatt and Milburn. Though no Chelsea player was near, they panicked and at a sudden lunge from both, the ball went rocketing into the net. The scoring was officially recorded as 'Froggatt and Milburn shared own goal'.

Chelsea fared only moderately in their Christmas encounters with Arsenal. They lost the first by a solitary goal at Highbury, and a late equaliser by O'Connell (after Bentley had missed yet another penalty) averted a holiday blank at Stamford Bridge on Boxing Day when, for the second time in the season, the gates were shut.

But on 1st January Chelsea showed the world how seriously they were taking their New Year resolutions. All five teams sent on the field were victorious, and in the five-two win at Bolton, Peter Sillett put an end to the penalty jinx. Not since October 1937 had Chelsea scored five in an away League match; curiously that last occasion was also at Bolton in a game drawn five-all. In addition to solving the penalty problem Sillett now captained the Young England team, and on 19th January in the familiar Stamford Bridge setting, he led them to a splendid victory by five-one over Italy in the first Intermediate International played in England. Blunstone also had a share in that triumph, scoring the third goal.

How Chelsea progressed to the Championship is shown by the following League table readings taken at the end of each month.

The Title Race - Month By Month									
	P	W	D	L	F	A	Pts	Pos	Leaders
Aug	4	2	2	0	6	4	6	6th	Preston
Sep	11	5	4	2	15	12	14	4th	WBA
Oct	16	5	5	6	24	25	15	12th	Wolves
Nov	20	7	7	6	34	31	21	11th	Wolves
Dec	25	10	8	7	46	37	28	5th	S'land
Jan	27	11	8	8	51	41	30	6th	Wolves
Feb	30	13	9	8	60	46	35	3rd	Wolves
Mar	36	17	10	9	71	52	44	1st	Chelsea
Apr	42	20	12	10	81	57	52	1st	Chelsea

Back to Chelsea. In the next match at home to Manchester City, Drake's men offered no semblance of solution to the much-publicised 'Revie Plan' and deservedly lost two-nil, but a draw on the Everton ground put them back in the running. This they followed by beating Newcastle at home. Twelve minutes from time Chelsea were leading four-nil. For no reason other than to remind us of the ways of old, the defence suddenly fell apart. Newcastle slapped in three goals and in a spirited finale were just denied an equaliser. It was Chelsea's first double against the Geordies and Bentley's first hat-trick after seven years with the club - against his old team.

A week later the Cup dream came to a slippery end in the fifth round. On a Notts County pitch resembling an ice-rink [pictured right], one goal sufficed to separate the teams. Chelsea's defence put up a worthy performance but not so the forwards, none of whom was prepared on the day to chance a shot when in sight of goal as Notts County's left-winger, Broadbent, did just after half-time.

Disappointing as it was, the Cup defeat may have been the catalyst for Chelsea going on to Championship triumph. The immediate reaction was to overrun Huddersfield four-one, and although beaten two-three at Villa Park on the first Saturday in March they did not concede another match until the race was won.

The turning point came in a rearranged match at West Bromwich on Wednesday, 9th March, attended by a mere 7,500. Snow lay on the pitch and there was doubt about the game being started. Chelsea wished it hadn't when they were two down at half time. Though Saunders sent home a twenty-yarder Chelsea were still losing one-two with ten minutes to go. Then things happened. Sillett belted a free-kick through the defensive wall to equalise. Seconds later he kicked the perfect penalty and in the last minute Bentley hoisted the score to four-two. Four remarkable goals in twenty-five minutes - three by defenders - and Chelsea were now in third place.

Over-anxiety crept into the following game, a goalless business against Blackpool which not even Stanley Matthews could save from utter mediocrity. Still, the point put Chelsea second, and the position was consolidated when Blunstone and O'Connell sent scoring shots past Bartram at Charlton's ground.

In four more days Chelsea were astride the football globe, winning by O'Connell's only goal at Cardiff. The news burst from the sporting columns onto the front pages, and "CHELSEA TOP FOR THE FIRST TIME IN 50 YEARS" read like the football writer's dream come true, except that Chelsea had occupied that exalted position twice before, in September 1922 and October 1937.

February 1955 — Chick Thomson in action on Notts County's frozen pitch

It had never happened at that advanced stage of the season, how-ever, and was enough to paralyse the London national newspaper indus-try for almost a month. Somebody even suggested that the strike-leader was an ardent Arsenal fan!

By beating Sunderland two-one at home in mid-week Chelsea length-ened the lead over Wolves to three points. A new left-wing had to be found because O'Connell was injured playing for Bishop Auckland the previous weekend, and Blunstone was required for training with the England team to meet Scotland. So Ted Drake tried an experiment with Peter Brabrook, a seventeen-year-old junior, at inside-left in his first big game partnered by Stan Willemse, who had been absent three weeks with influenza. Brabrook centred the ball that Sunderland's left-back turned into his own net after eleven minutes, and straight away Willemse, to his unconcealed delight, right-footed a second goal when Parsons dropped a corner at his feet.

Next day the team set off on their third pilgrimage of the season to Broadstairs, now to prepare for the supreme effort. At Tottenham four days later [pictured right] Chelsea were without Blunstone and Armstrong, both helping England to a seven-two victory over the Scots at Wembley, but twice The Blues hit back from behind to win four-two. McNichol scored two, Wicks brought off a surprise header from Willemse's corner-kick and finally Sillett obliged yet again from the penalty spot. This was indeed a fighting Chelsea, with the 'fight' over-emphasised for many of the Spurs supporters. The last three goals came in a thirteen-minute burst, leaving behind the club's First Division scor-ing record set at seventy-four the previous season.

So to Easter with a four-point lead. Wolves lay second with two matches in hand, closely followed by Portsmouth, Manchester United and Manchester City. Chelsea's holiday fixtures, two compared with the three being played by most clubs, were both at home, and the players knew that nothing short of three points would be considered satisfac-tory. Remembering that Chelsea had not won a match for seven Easters, it was no light assignment.

Good Friday's display against Sheffield United caused gravest con-cern, for Chelsea could only draw one-all through a goal by Parsons fifteen minutes from the end and never once suggested Championship pedigree. But the contrast between the Chelsea of Good Friday and the Chelsea of Easter Saturday defied all reason. It needed to, for that game against Wolverhampton was virtually the Championship decider.

Forty-five minutes before kick-off, mounted police stood firm against a human tide in front of the gates that had been closed with 75,000 spectators already crammed into the stadium. There seemed to be as

April 1955 – Roy Bentley goes close during the 4-2 win at White Hart Lane

many people outside the ground as in, where the terraces were packed solid and every hoarding had become a grandstand of sorts. Ten minutes before the teams appeared thousands jumped the rails and claimed squatters' rights on the greyhound track, leaving police and officials powerless to intervene.

Into such an electric atmosphere on a sunny afternoon stepped the teams, first Wolves, then Chelsea, for a game that was to reach and in some ways exceed all expectations and earn a place among the greatest played at Stamford Bridge.

Wolves had had no Good Friday fixture, yet Chelsea looked the fresher side, attacking with such zest and purpose that at least two goals should have arrived by half-time. Instead the score sheet stayed blank, for which Wolves could thank Williams more than anyone else. Three of his saves, from a Parsons power-drive, Bentley's flying header and Sillett's cannon from thirty-five yards, were stamped world-class, but not even Williams should have survived one minute before the interval. Blunstone's diagonal pass over Shorthouse sent Parsons clear at speed, and ten yards from the target the winger cut the ball back to give Bentley an easy, wide-angled chance. Only Williams stood between Bentley and the rigging, but a hurried shot was stopped and the ball rolled gently into grateful hands.

Besides the excellence of Wolves' goalkeeper, the match so far had produced some notable half-back play, especially from Wicks and Saunders for Chelsea and the persistent young Flowers for the visitors, with Billy Wright scarcely less impressive. From the thirtieth minute Wolves had Swinbourne limping with a wrenched knee; gamely he carried on while colleagues did all they could to mask the gap.

Chick Thomson's first save did not come until the second half, when wee Hancocks exploded a free-kick from forty yards. Faster and faster play ebbed and flowed with Parsons threatening to win the day, several times he wriggled through Wolves' defence, only to find a Wolves defender instead of one of his own forwards pouncing on the vital last pass. When another 'gift', this time O'Connell, was declined, allowing Williams to gather from five yards, the situation seemed ripe for Wolves to play up their good fortune and grab the points.

Then, a quarter of an hour from the end - high drama. From twelve yards O'Connell drove hard and true for the top right-hand corner and as Williams clawed the air, behind him on the line rose Wright, arms extended above his blond head, to turn the ball behind. In that split-second the crowd became a screaming mass; nor were Chelsea's players in any doubt that the ball had been handled. They swarmed around referee J. W. Malcolm of Leicester, among them Willemse, who reached the scene in record time to add thunder to the general appeal. At first the referee indicated a corner-kick. Then he went to the touchline to consult the linesman, and after seconds that seemed like minutes he pointed to the penalty spot.

This was the moment for the young giant, Peter Sillett, to command the stage - Sillett who had kicked three goals from three penalty-kicks since other Chelsea players had muffed five in a row. None of them had been as important as this. Williams stood, a tense figure on is line, as the ball was placed for this kick of destiny. Then, permitting himself one pace more than his customary two, Sillett connected with his right foot and the ball flashed under Williams and into the net [pictured right]. Its very speed baffled the eye, this penalty with the will and seemingly force of 75,000 right feet behind it. And as the crowd's roar broke the silence and colleagues converged in congratulation, Sillett temporarily disappeared from view.

With time and a goal against them, Wolves threw everything into attack. They switched Hancocks to centre-forward - the smallest man on the field against Wicks, the tallest - and how nearly the little fellow with the outsize heart and a kick to match went to wiping out Chelsea's lead. To Hancocks any chance within forty yards could be turned to account, and when he danced past two men to within less than half that

April 1955 — Peter Sillett burries the ball in the Wolves net during the 'must win' match

distance Thomson's hopes were small indeed, but the shot that fizzed past, smashed against the far post and Saunders was there to clear.

Soon Chelsea hearts fluttered again. This time Hancocks was obstructed in the penalty area, and in massed resistance all eleven Chelsea players lined up to face the indirect free-kick. Preliminaries over, Wilshaw flicked the ball aside for Hancocks to let fly, and we breathed again as his shot curled away past the distant upright.

Watched by another three thousand people who had burst into the ground when the gates were opened ready for the exodus, Chelsea held on under almost constant assault. And when the whistle sounded, hundreds took it as the signal to leap on to the field and join their heroes. The last player to escape the throng was the one who had done most to thwart Chelsea that day - Williams, expressing a scowl of torment and dismay even as the stands rose to applaud his magnificent performance.

And while boys in their dozen kicked imaginary penalty goals at either end of the field, we moved for home, daring to believe that we had seen Wolves, the retiring Champions, beaten by Chelsea, the new.

Chelsea next faced their last real challengers - Portsmouth at Fratton Park, a ground that had not been kind to them in previous years. With O'Connell gaining an Amateur Cup-winner's medal with Bishop Auckland, two-nil conquerors of Hendon at Wembley that afternoon, Stubbs reappeared... and maintained his doubtful reputation as the 'unluckiest forward on the books'. In the first half a tremendous drive by him was headed off the line, and in the second he was given off-

April 1955 – The Captains shake hands before Chelsea's title decider against Wednesday

side after shooting what even the Portsmouth players were prepared to accept as a good enough goal. Despite thrills at either end, that was the only shot to find the net.

So to Chelsea's final home game, in one way unfortunate as it threw together the top team and the bottom, Sheffield Wednesday, who were booked for Division Two. No longer burdened with the fight for survival and in a mood of carefree abandon, the Hillsborough men had won their two previous games, and the state of anxiety now switched to Chelsea, who could clinch the Championship by winning this match.

A 51,000 crowd assembled in readiness to acclaim the new Champions, but for everyone present, the memory will remain not of the match itself but of the scenes afterwards. Too many of the Chelsea players were understandably given to nervous tension for the side to do itself proper justice. Among the exceptions was Parsons, who chose this hour as one of his greatest, and headed the only first-half goal. Early in the second half Wednesday lost their goalkeeper, McIntosh, injured in a collision with Bentley. Their misfortune continued when a drive by Saunders struck Sewell high on the arm and without appeal, referee W. Ling, in his last League match, gave a penalty. Sillett kidded everyone by side-footing this one into the goal, and ten minutes from time Chelsea scored again. Parsons swivelled to meet Blunstone's centre at the near post and guided his shot low towards Curtis. It looked an easy ball for the deputy goalkeeper, but slipped under his hands and into the net.

Champions — Ted Drake and the players on the balcony after securing their crown

That was it, three-nil, and all that remained was to hear the result of the Cardiff versus Portsmouth match which had started fifteen minutes later than Chelsea's. Across the greyhound track and onto the pitch, excited crowds formed a huge semi-circle in front of the main stand. Then came the news: 'Cardiff one, Portsmouth one' and a whoop of joy went up. Chelsea were Champions! Champions in their year of Golden Jubilee.

From the eldest supporter, worn with the years of waiting for that moment, to the youngest Chelsea follower, came the call for the players and the man behind the players. Photographers jostled for positions from which to take a picture that had been denied them fifty years. Hastily a microphone was installed in the directors' box; then, to tumultuous cheering, the team made their triumphant appearance, followed by Ted Drake.

First to the microphone was chairman Joe Mears, unashamedly wiping a tear from his eyes. He spoke not without emotion. 'I would like to thank everyone for the wonderful ovation you have given us today and for your support all through the season. It is not for me to say more than a few words. You want to hear from Roy and the boys, and from the one and only Ted...'

His words were lost among cheers as Ted Drake stepped forward, his team leading the applause from either side. 'This is the happiest moment of my life,' said Ted. 'At the start of the season I was asked if we would

Ted Drake and the Chelsea Directors proudly display the season's trophy haul

win the Cup. I thought we might, but I thought we had a greater chance of winning the Championship. I congratulate all the boys and every one of my staff, office, training and playing. Right throughout they are one and all CHELSEA.'

Then Ted brought Roy Bentley, team captain, to the microphone to say: 'On behalf of the boys, thank you all. There is no need for me to say how pleased we all are to win the Championship, but we are pleased, too, for your sakes, because you have been behind us in other years when we needed your support. From the bottom of our hearts thank you very much.' And as he finished, Bentley produced possibly his finest stroke of captaincy by introducing Johnny Harris, Chelsea's oldest serving player, captain for many years and twelfth man on this as on recent match-days. Harris, touched by Roy's gesture, said, 'I am so happy to be with all the boys on this happiest day of my life now that the Championship has come to Chelsea...'

And with the cheers of the crowd ringing in their ears, and to the cry of 'We want Rabbit!' - Eric Parsons - the new Champions passed from view to the champagne awaiting them in the dressing room. Half an hour later they filed into the gymnasium where the BBC, anticipating the events now accomplished had fixed a microphone. By now news of Chelsea's Championship had gone round the world, and listeners to 'Sports Report' heard the voices of Ted Drake, Roy Bentley and the hero of this day and many others, Eric Parsons.

Then the players, their wives and close friends of the club were invited into the directors' private room for the kind of family gathering that Ted Drake could never have imagined when he began the Chelsea transformation in 1952. His face reflected the joy and pride in his heart as he read out telegrams of congratulation that were already pouring in as evidence of the affection with which Chelsea were regarded throughout football.

Even in that atmosphere of celebration some found it hard to grasp that Chelsea were Champions, that this was their day of days. So the final night editions were bought (the newspaper strike having ended two days before) and the written word, big and bold, was there for all to see.

For the last match of an historic season Chelsea went to Old Trafford to play Manchester United. By remarkable coincidence Chelsea's first game with Ted Drake in command was on the same ground when Manchester United were League Champions. Now that honour had come to Chelsea, and as Roy Bentley led them out, the home team applauded them onto the field while the band played 'See the conquering heroes come'.

Chelsea's field of conquest in their Jubilee Year extended far beyond the Football League, for three other League trophies went to Stamford Bridge. The Reserves won the Football Combination, the 'A' team headed the Metropolitan League and the Juniors took the South-East Counties League. Truly, in every way, Chelsea were Champions.

Albert Sewell

Frank
Blunstone

I don't know why I went to Chelsea really, there were a lot of First Division clubs in for me at the time including Newcastle, Sunderland and Arsenal who were all massive clubs. They all wanted me to sign for them, yet for some reason I went to Stamford Bridge. I'd had the chance to move on from Crewe a while before Chelsea's offer came in for me though, Stoke, who were a big force in the First Division themselves, made a bid of £15,000 to Crewe for myself and team-mate Johnny King. But I wouldn't go there even though it was just up the road and they had the likes of Stanley Matthews playing for them.

Then one day the Crewe manager, Harry Catterick, called me in to say that Ted Drake, who like Harry was a former England centre-forward, had made a bid to take me to Chelsea and would I like to go? Well, I think it was the thought of moving to the city that made me say yes almost straight away and I felt that I'd have a better chance of making it in London than I would have had in Stoke - especially of being picked for England. I didn't hesitate, I went straight down and signed.

In those days the manager didn't speak to the players about joining their club, all the discussions took place between officials, so the first time I met Ted Drake was on the Thursday I travelled down to London to sign. I vividly remember travelling back on the train and excitedly thinking, 'I've just signed for Chelsea!' Then it started to hit home what I'd let myself in for - a big club with big crowds in a big ground - and me, a kid of only eighteen from Crewe. I had to leave my eight brothers and five sisters behind and move to a city where I didn't know anybody. It was a daunting prospect.

Looking back now, I didn't have a clue what I was letting myself in for, every time I got on the underground I got lost and I had to go and live in digs after living at home all my life. It was a life changing move more than a life style changing move, my signing-on fee for Chelsea was £10, which I got taxed on, and my wages were £12 a week. Crewe were happy though, they'd received £8500 for me in an era when the record transfer was £18,000, which I guess in relative terms is the equivalent of about £12 million today.

My landlady was a woman called Mrs. Scott who lived at 11, Britannia Road, Chelsea, just up the road from The Britannia pub. Few people in football today would believe me when I say that young centre-forward Bobby Smith, who went on to win the double at Spurs, and myself had to share the same double bed. I spent half the night fighting for the bedclothes - can you imagine that happening today? The club were very good to us though, we used to get free tickets for the local theatres and cinemas and there were snooker tables at Stamford Bridge, so we had a good time away from training, but the stadium became the centre of our lives. I would imagine that the current Chelsea players only see the ground on match-days.

We were only eighteen and nineteen, so at the time these perks were important to us. The club also gave us a season ticket so we travelled free on the underground around London, plus, in the first season I was there, all our meals were supplied from the restaurant inside Stamford Bridge. After that we were given food vouchers to eat in a café near The Bridge called Annabelle's, which I think is still there, or to a little Italian restaurant down the Fulham Road near Barclays Bank. Chelsea did as much for us as they were allowed, but they couldn't pay us any extra or give us any more because the maximum wage rules were in force still and regulations were very strict.

I was very homesick when I first arrived, but Ted Drake was very good about it and used to give me an extra day off some Mondays so I could get home and see my family for longer. After a while I made more friends in London and my outlook widened, so the visits home became less frequent, but it was a big help at the time for Ted to be allowing me to get back to Crewe as much as I could.

Ted Drake didn't promise me anything when I joined, although he said that he thought I had a good future in the game and he wanted me to play. I thought that was fair enough. I knew it was up to me to prove myself at a bigger club and I was confident enough to be able to make my mark at Stamford Bridge, but I wasn't able to go straight into the first team.

Chelsea had an FA Cup Sixth Round tie with Birmingham the weekend after I arrived, which we lost 4-0, but I'd already been Cup-tied with Crewe in a previous round, so Ted Drake asked me if I'd like tickets to watch the Cup match, or travel with the 'A' team? I said that I'd prefer to be playing rather than watching, so I travelled down to Chelmsford City where we won 6-2. I remember Dave Sexton was playing for Chelmsford, which seems like a huge coincidence when I look back, because Dave not only became a very good friend of mine, he also emerged as Chelsea's most successful manager of all time for his achievements between 1967 and 1974.

I didn't have to wait long for my first game though and I made my debut for the first team on March 14th, 1953 but the match came at the end of possibly the worst week of my life. I'll always remember the training session at Stamford Bridge one Monday morning, half way through I was called to one side and told that The Boss wanted to talk to me in his office - straight away. I was mystified, I was sure I hadn't done anything wrong, so I had a bath, got changed, then went up to Ted Drake's office. As I walked in he said, "Frank, sit down, I'll get somebody to make you a

1950 — Blunstone [bottom left] in his blazer poses with the England schoolboys

cup of tea." I thought to myself, "aye-aye, what's happened here?" Then he told me that my eldest brother, John, had been killed in a motorcycle accident that morning. Poor old Ted had to tell me news that still upsets me today. I was told to go straight back home to Crewe on the train as the funeral was on the Thursday afternoon.

That evening, a few hours after we'd buried my brother, I received a phone call from Ted to tell me that he'd decided to pick me to play in the first team that coming Saturday. He told me that I didn't have to play if I didn't want to, that he understood my situation, but he wanted me to make my debut. I asked my Mum what she thought I should do. She told me right away that I should play, that my brother John would have wanted me to, so that's what I did. I ran out for my first Chelsea match against Tottenham and scored the equaliser - it was meant to be.

To be honest I found that I coped with the step up in levels quite easily considering the week I'd had - even with Alf Ramsey marking me at right back for Tottenham that day I didn't find it that difficult. From then on, I never looked back.

I was one of the final additions to Ted Drake's title winning side, Peter Sillett had signed from Southampton just before me, as had Stan Wicks from Reading, so the majority of the Championship jigsaw had already been assembled before I arrived. The only players brought in following my transfer were Jim Lewis and Seamus O'Connell, but they were amateurs and we only saw them on match-days.

It was quite unusual to have amateurs back then, but Chelsea seemed to sign quite a few of them. Ted had also signed a left winger called Miles Spector from Finchley and Derek Saunders from Walthamstow Avenue. Mind you, people called them amateurs, but they were earning a lot more than us professionals because they were earning wages from their Monday-to-Friday jobs, then Chelsea were paying them an appearance fee, so they were doing very well indeed.

There wasn't much training either if the truth were known. We practiced most days, but nothing like today and every Monday morning we had to get off the pitch at Stamford Bridge at eleven o'clock because of the Greyhound trials around the perimeter, which was utter madness.

We had some very good, promising, young players in our team, as well as some more experienced heads like John Harris, but I don't think many people were seriously considering us as title contenders when the 1954-55 season started. In the early part of the season we were always well placed, but never really got any higher than mid-table. Being behind seemed to be the norm with us, but often we'd come back to win, that was the spirit of the side. It seemed as if we needed to be given a jolt before we started to play to our potential and to get us going.

The game that stands out in my mind, the turning point where we started to emerge as serious contenders, was a re-arranged midweek game away at West Brom in March 1955. Les Stubbs won the game for us that day, not because of his brilliant play or anything like that, his less subtle skills were called upon. Les was a wholehearted player, somebody who you'd always want in your team and that freezing afternoon he was having a right go at their goalie, a player by the name of Sanders.

Les was niggling at him all through the game, every time the goalie caught the ball Les would give him a nudge, it happened so often that in the end Sanders lost his temper with Les, he kicked the ball away, turned around, then booted Les. The referee saw the kick and immediately blew his whistle and pointed to the spot for a penalty. We had been two goals down in the snow and really struggling before Derek Saunders pulled one back with ten minutes to go, then John Sillett scored from a free kick to draw level - but that penalty was the turning point and I don't think we would have won otherwise.

That match was played out in terrible conditions and would never have started today. Thick snow lay on the ground and passing became a lottery. You'd play what you thought was a good through-ball, then it would stop dead in some snow and you'd have to set off after it and try and win the ball all over again. They were farcical conditions really, although not as bad as an F.A. Cup tie at Tranmere in 1962. The Cup tie was the only fixture in the whole of England that remained on and there was so much snow it was dangerous. Frank Upton was going mad that day for Chelsea and almost had a big fight with John King, who eventually went on to be manager at Prenton Park. Luckily we drew 2-2 and beat them in the replay.

The win at West Brom was important in another way because the division was so tight, if we'd lost, Chelsea could have dropped a few places and that could have affected our belief. We couldn't afford to fall too far behind Wolves and to have lost two points in the Championship race would have been a massive blow at that time. So from that day I started to believe that we could be Champions, March 9th 1955 was the turning point as far as I was concerned and I started to get really excited about the run-in to the end of the season.

Ted Drake's attitude remained the same despite the pressure, I didn't get the impression he was getting any more confident about the title. Drake was a gentleman, but he did have a bit of a temper on him at times and I remember a fair few cups of tea being thrown around the dressing room at half-time when he was less than happy with us. But he was very enthusiastic too, I can remember more than one occasion when he came down to watch a training session and he'd come on the pitch in his suit and shoes and try and correct somebody. He'd shout "no, no, no, head the ball like this", before jumping up and nodding a crossed ball into the net. Then he would walk off again covered in mud.

Ted was no tactician though, but there weren't really many tactics in those days. All Eric Parsons and myself on the other flank were told to do as wingers was to beat the full-back, get the ball to the bye-line and pull a good cross back for one of the strikers to nod down or get on the end of. We were encouraged to take people on and get past defenders, something that doesn't seem to be done so much today. There was never any pressure on me to score more goals, Ted Drake was just happy for me to set up as many as I could, although I did score three during the 1954-55 season. That Chelsea side was a good attacking team.

I think that's why the games were more high scoring back then, most teams were always going flat out for the win, playing for a draw was a rarity, which is surprising I think. It should be more important to win today as there are more points up for grabs - there were only two points for a win in those days remember.

One game from the Championship season, which really demonstrates the attacking nature of footballers in that era, was the home match with Manchester United. I wasn't involved as I was out injured, but for a game to finish Chelsea five, Manchester United six, shows how both teams were going flat out to win. But that was just one of many high-scoring encounters that year. Winning 4-3 at Molineux was another fantastic game to play in.

I was doing my National Service with the Army that season too, which meant I was away from training and the ground for much of the time - I was being paid one pound and eight shillings per week by the Army and another pound by Chelsea, plus six pounds per match. You had to play to get the extra money though, if you didn't play you only got a pound. But that wasn't Chelsea's fault, they were the F.A. rules then. Chelsea's Assistant Secretary, Harry Green, used to help bump up the youngsters' expenses when he could, but I remember we were so honest and naïve that I couldn't understand why he always claimed a dinner on the train from Aldershot for me when I never ate on the journey once!

Everyone of my age had to do their National Service and when Ted Drake signed me in February 1953 he asked me if I'd enlisted in the forces yet. I told him that I had and was due to serve in the North Staffordshire Regiment. Ted couldn't believe that as a footballer, Crewe had allowed me to join what was basically a marching regiment - he said "no way" and asked his secretary, Mrs. Metcalf, to phone Colonel Mitchell at the Army Football Association right there and then. Ted was on first name terms with the Colonel and he said, "hello Gerry, I've just signed the boy Blunstone from Crewe and I'd like him based with The Medics in Crookham near Aldershot..." There was no problem whatsoever and that's exactly where I ended up. My room-mate, Bobby Smith, was in The Medics too, but somehow Ted Drake had wangled it for him to be based at Millbank, on Embankment in the centre of London. Smithy didn't even have to leave our digs! So, although I was playing for Chelsea, I was based in barracks for two years and very much in the Army. I was in charge of latrine duties, the glamorous job of making sure the toilets were clean! Because I was out and about playing football all over the place I was assigned a job that had no responsibility at all.

It was an amazing thing, people talk about how many games that modern day footballers are forced to play, but at the time I was playing four games a week. I had to play for my depot team, the Southern Command team, the Army team, plus, of course, Chelsea on the Saturday. On top of those I was picked to play for my country. Quite often we had a depot match on a Friday afternoon too, less than twenty-four hours before I was due to be playing in the First Division. I used to try and take it a bit easy in the depot matches, but usually one of the opposition side would single me out and try and nobble me because I was a Chelsea player. So pride would take over and I ended up trying to show the buggers, then you start playing and chasing the ball around like an idiot! Sometimes I'd walk off knackered, then remember I had a far more important game the next day.

There were a number of times that I played injured for Chelsea after picking up knocks in other games, but I wanted to play, I also needed the extra £6. You always knew at the back of your mind that if you missed a game there was another player who would come in and you may not get your place in the side back for a while. All those games caused me to suffer a lot of trouble with my shins, they ached almost all of the time and Jack Oxberry, the Chelsea trainer, reckoned I had rheumatism and stopped me from training. These pains carried on for a long time, then one day, when we were playing Tottenham away in the F.A. Cup in 1957, I got a smack early on which broke my leg. They X-rayed it at the ground and said they couldn't find anything wrong with it, so I remember my uncle had to carry me home on his back to his little flat in Highbury where I was staying when I came out of .

I was in so much pain that night that when morning came around I got straight on the phone to Jack Oxberry again to tell him I was really in trouble, that I couldn't put any weight on the leg and I was in agony. He sent a car over to fetch me straight away, but it took another two visits to the hospital and another three days of pain before a nurse spotted a fracture at the back of my leg and put me in plaster. A week or so

April 1955 — Blunstone warms up before the 2-1 defeat at Old Trafford

February 1955 — Frank Blunstone takes on the Huddersfield defence in a 4-1 home win

March 1955 — Blunstone delivers a corner during the snowy 4-2 win at West Brom

later I received a phone call from a specialist at the hospital who said they had held a meeting about my injury - after asking a few questions he came to the conclusion that I'd possibly been playing with a hair-line-fractured leg for a year. It was only the Spurs defender's tackle that eventually aggravated it further otherwise it probably would have gone untreated for even longer. When my fracture did heal enough to play in the first team again, my leg snapped in exactly the same place in my first game back! That's an example of how we were expected to just keep playing and of how your body simply can't cope with that many games.

Because of my commitments away from Chelsea, and bearing in mind I was injured and missed the beginning of the season, I still played over a hundred competitive matches during the 1954-55 season. The Army team had first refusal over anyone else, I even had to miss a Chelsea game to play for the depot in the Hampshire Senior Cup - a First Round game against Sandown on the Isle of Wight. Tosh Chamberlain, who played for Fulham and became my closest friend in the Army, was injured so he thought he wouldn't have to travel with us, but because of his experience he was made trainer for the day and had to get on the ferry over there with the rest of us.

There was a full-back playing for Sandown who had singled me out because I was 'the Chelsea star' and he clattered into me twice, really hard. The first time I was chopped down Tosh came running over to me and helped me up and made sure I was okay to carry on, but on the second occasion I remember seeing Tosh run straight past me and grab their defender. My mate threatened to smash his face in if he did it again. I wondered what the hell he was doing as I lay on the ground clutching my ankle. The referee had a right go at him, then the crowd got on his back too, so in the end Tosh was arguing and falling out with everyone. Things became almost farcical then, from being two-nil up we ended up drawing the match two-all and were facing the prospect of extra time and missing the last ferry back to the mainland.

At the final whistle Tosh marched back onto the pitch and straight over to the referee telling the official, "there's no way we're playing extra time, we've got a boat to catch!" The referee was having none of it though and he made us play on, but fifteen minutes in he blew his whistle and abandoned the game because it was almost pitch black. On marched Tosh again and had another bust-up with the referee. Luckily there was another ferry, but we didn't get back to the barracks until the early hours and we had to make a return trip for a replay - which we won four-one.

Because of National Service there were some fantastic players in that Army team at the time, including eight full internationals. Scotland and

Sunderland's Bill Fraser in goal, Manchester City and England's Jimmy Meadows, Tottenham and Wales' Mel Hopkins and Blackburn Rovers and England Captain Ronnie Clayton. We also had Albert Quixall who played for Manchester United and England, Mel Charles for Swansea and Wales, Phil Woosnam, Wales and West Ham, then there was me - Chelsea and England. Our Army side was even invited up to Glasgow Rangers for an exhibition match to open their new floodlights - there was a crowd of over fifty thousand to see us win two-nil.

The trouble with that workload, on top of my day-to-day Army work, was that it became very tiring mentally as well as physically. It was certainly a season of extremes for me, one day I could be cleaning out the toilets in the Army barracks, or playing in what were no more than park kick-abouts, then I had the contrast of being picked for the full England team and winning the First Division Championship.

I'll never forget being called up to represent my country for the first time. I got back to barracks on the Sunday evening, after our three-all draw at Roker Park [photo right], and had no idea what was about to happen the next morning over breakfast in the Sergeant's Mess. As I sat down to eat, Tosh Chamberlain told me that The Colonel wanted to see me straight away. Tosh was a real joker and there was no way I was going to fall for his tricks first thing in the morning, "get lost", I said to him. Tosh replied, "Frank, on my life, I'm not kidding..." and he looked so serious and concerned himself that I knew he was being straight with me and it wasn't another goose chase.

So off I went to The Colonel's office, I knocked on the door and I heard him boom; "Ah Blunstone, come in. You've been picked to play for England on Wednesday, go and get a pass and make sure you're back here on Thursday morning at eight o'clock". That was it, no 'well done Frank', all he seemed interested in was that I was back on camp almost straight away.

Ronnie Allen from West Brom had been picked ahead of me originally, but he got injured in their game on the Saturday and had to pull out. That gave me my big chance, but I had a touch of the flu. I arrived at Hendon Hall Hotel on the Monday evening and spoke to the England Manager, Walter Winterbottom. As I wasn't feeling very well he told me to dose myself up with medicine and not to train with the team the next day, but I was desperate to play, there was no way I was going to miss that game against Wales. Chelsea Captain, Roy Bentley, was there with me which was a big help, to have a familiar face in the camp is very reassuring, he was a father figure really. Roy had a great game against Wales, scoring all three England goals and his record for his country was hugely impressive.

November 1954 — Action from the 3–3 draw at Sunderland's Roker Park

Training at Stamford Bridge — Frank and the lads set off on a long run

August 1954 — Bentley's goal in the opening day draw at Leicester City

April 1955 — Wolves' Billy Wright punches the ball over to concede a penalty at The Bridge

I was very nervous when I walked out at Wembley, 95,000 people were there to see us take on the Welsh, but as soon as the game started I forgot the importance of the occasion and tried to enjoy the game. It was a shame I wasn't feeling quite 100%, as I could have played better, but all fourteen members of my family were there to see me play and it was a wonderful night in my life. I felt it was a great honour for my parents as well as me, it was special for them to be there. I was also part of the England side which beat Scotland seven-two later that season.

The Scotland game is something I never let Tommy Docherty, who played at right-half that day, forget when I joined him at Manchester United later in my career. Tommy always liked to have the last word and was always very quick to get his point of view across. I rarely won when there was a difference of opinion between us, so whenever I could see I was losing an argument I used to say, "hold on, do you remember when we played you at Wembley? What was the score?" "Eff-off", he used to tell me, but it put him off what he was saying so it must have been a very sore point. I hope it still is too! Unfortunately my leg breaks restricted my England career to five games, which was a shame because I felt I became a better player with age. I would have loved to have played for my country again when I was twenty-eight as I know I would have performed so much better.

Although I was in the team for Chelsea's first game of the season, a one-all draw at Leicester [pictured top left], I was out injured from then until the beginning of November, returning for the three-all draw at home to Sunderland. It was pointed out to me fairly recently that my return to the side coincided with a change in fortunes for Chelsea and results improved.

Although I wouldn't claim to have turned things around single-handedly, everything that was achieved was always a team effort, but I remember that a run of four straight defeats was stopped and Chelsea started to pick up points again. We scored twenty-one goals in just seven games between then and Christmas.

Doing the double over Wolves was some achievement too, winning four-three at Molineux was unbelievable, but the home game, in front of 75,000 at Stamford Bridge, where a Peter Sillett penalty won it one-nil, was the real grudge match and ultimate title decider between the two sides. The four points we took from Stan Cullis' side was the margin that divided us from the runners-up in the end. Wolves had a great side, five of them were internationals and the match at Stamford Bridge was a very tense affair.

We almost had to settle for a draw, though, if it wasn't for the linesman spotting an incident the referee missed, we would never have been awarded our penalty. We were attacking and Seamus O'Connell hit a great shot that looked destined for the top corner, then we saw Billy Wright's fist [pictured previous page] come up and punch the ball over the bar. The referee obviously thought that their goalie, Bert Williams, had made the save, but everybody else, bar him, knew it was a clear hand ball - so you can imagine the Chelsea players' reaction when the referee pointed for a corner - there was mayhem! Fortunately the linesman had continued to hold his flag up to get the referee's attention. We told the referee to go and speak to the lino (or more colourful words to the same effect) and eventually, to everyone's relief, he gave the penalty.

What a responsibility Peter Sillett had in taking that spot kick. Peter was normally as calm as anything in those situations, he'd just walk up from two or three paces back and side-foot the ball into the bottom corner of the net, but not that day! Goal-less, Stamford Bridge packed to the rafters and against our closest title rivals... Peter must have gone back about twenty yards before running up and smashing the ball with all his might - it flew past Bert Williams. The atmosphere among the fans was very tense too, there wasn't the greatest atmosphere, but the players were so far away from the spectators because of the dog track around the edge of the pitch that it was sometimes difficult to hear them. But in my opinion that result showed we could defend and grind results out when we had to.

I was very nervous before that home game with Wolves, it was such a make or break fixture. We all knew that there was so much riding on our shoulders and that one mistake could prove so costly. There was no love lost between the two clubs then and a lot of the ill feeling stemmed from a feud between Ted Drake and his opposite number at Molineux, Stan Cullis. They had a punch-up on the touchline up there the season before when we'd been thrashed eight-one. We really struggled that day! We'd lost Bobby Smith and Ron Greenwood through injury and were eight-nil down with only nine men on the pitch.

The bust up came shortly after Chelsea were awarded a penalty, Roy Bentley stepped up to take the spot-kick but Bert Williams saved it. Fortunately the ball rebounded to Roy and he scored, but at the re-start Cullis was on the touchline shouting at the Wolves players to push on and score more goals. Ted obviously got the right hump at this and the next thing the two managers were squaring up to each other. We got revenge for that back at Stamford Bridge though and won four-two in front of sixty thousand fans - then we did the double over them during the Championship season. I know that Ted Drake wanted to beat Wolverhampton Wanderers as much as he wanted to win the title and he was delighted to achieve both.

There was a lot of newspaper talk back then about how much we relied on our team spirit, how we used to battle for results, but there was a hell of a lot more skill in that side than some gave us credit for. Four of us became England internationals, Ken Armstrong, Roy Bentley, Peter Sillett and myself, which showed the calibre of the team. In the mid-50s an England squad only consisted of eleven players, not the twenty-two plus we see today, and there were no subs and no reserves. It was a hell of a job to get picked, so to have so many players from our Chelsea team selected was an amazing achievement.

There were others in that side that should have been called up too, Eric Parsons was as good a winger as there was back then. Eric was so unlucky at the time because Stanley Mathews and Tom Finney were both still around. That was the pedigree of player he was competing with.

But team spirit was obviously essential too, you have to have players who are prepared to fight and battle, but you don't win the Championship if you're a bad side do you? Whoever played us that season knew that they'd been in a game, nobody ever shirked and if we did lose, we went down giving a hundred percent.

Another thing that needs to be remembered about the Championship team was the importance of having a good goalkeeper at the back, Chelsea were lucky to have two, Charlie [Chick] Thompson and Bill Robertson. Charlie was very athletic, tall and skinny, Bill was big and hard - but we felt comfortable with either in goal and it was just down to injuries as to who played. If Chick was in the side then he'd keep his place until he got injured, then Bill would be the regular until something happened to him, then Chick would be back in for a while. That's what it was like in most positions though.

Stan Wicks was another pivotal player I thought and replaced Ron Greenwood at centre-back. That swap made a big difference to the side. Ron was a good thinker and a nice man, that was demonstrated through his success in football management, but he wasn't the best tackler in the world. He intercepted forwards well and knew where they were going to take the ball, so he could be there waiting, but more often than not he'd back off too much when he should have just got a tackle in. Once it became clear that Ted Drake had decided to stick with Stan, Ron Greenwood wanted to leave and he moved to Fulham before the end of the season. With only a handful of games to go some people may have thought it was a strange time to lose an experienced and respected player, but Ted knew that John Harris could play at right-back or centre-back, so there was still cover for injuries in the run-in.

In my opinion Wicksy was a brilliant centre-half and he should have played for England too. At 6ft 4in he had a huge presence, as did his

April 1955 – Blunstone [far right] listens to Ted Drake's famous Championship speech

defensive partner Stan Willemse. Boy was Stan hard, he took no prisoners on the football pitch and when I arrived Ted appointed Stan as my on-the-pitch minder. If the full-back got a bit naughty with me, Stan would have a word with them and make it obvious it wasn't in their best interests to do the same again. Don't get me wrong, I could look after myself and if I had to I would, but it was nice having Stan around too!

Stan Willemse was a naturally left-footed player and gave a great balance to the team, he was quick, he was hard and he was perfect for that position. Peter Sillett at right back was class too, strong, quick and read the game well. At right-half was Ken Armstrong, he was a beautiful footballer, another good, attacking player. Ken was always confident on the ball and although he may not have been the keenest tackler in the world, Ken contributed a huge amount to our Chelsea team.

It makes me laugh that we seemed to have so many 'hard' players along the left hand side of the pitch, because Derek Saunders was another tough, rough defender who would always win you the ball. Les Stubbs was inside-left, another 100%er who gave us everything and chased the ball all day. I remember Les giving Tottenham's Danny Blanchflower a tough old time that season, getting stuck into him in an attempt to stop him from playing as we all knew he could. Danny was a truly great player, but in the end Blanchflower turned round to the referee and shouted "have a word with this fella will you?" and Les walked right up to him and replied, "I may not be able to play, but I can stop you playing!" It seemed the perfect blend, there was a lot of determination and fight, but equally there was a lot of skill and creativity.

Then there was John Harris, or Gentleman John as some people called him off the pitch - John never swore, was a lay-preacher and the oldest player in the squad. He used to share a room with me on away trips because the manager thought he'd be a good influence on me, but John was a very dour Scotsman who used to try and instill his playing ethic of "forewarned, foretold" into me. He used to repeat that saying over and over, "forewarned, foretold", but I think he was just trying to justify his style of play. I lost count of the amount of times I saw him leave an opponent in a heap after going in for a challenge with John Harris and his motto was all about letting your opposite number know who was in control. He was a dirty bugger, sometimes an attack would break down and you'd turn around to defend and their centre-forward would be flat out on the grass where John had hit him without warning.

Out on the right wing was Eric Parsons who had the season of his life in 1954-55, he was outstanding and he was so quick they called him The Rabbit. Ted Drake made me train with Eric to try and get me to run quicker, but I could never get near him and I wasn't slow. After twenty yards he'd be another ten yards ahead of me. The manager thought that running with him would help pull me out, but it used to frustrate and embarrass me, he was too quick and I know he used to toy with me, pretending to let me keep up for a while before showing me his heels. Inside Eric on the right was John McNichol who was a good Scottish ball player and another very skilful footballer. Peter Brabrook, who went on to play more than two hundred and fifty games for Chelsea, also made a handful of appearances during the season.

I was out on the left flank and always thought I gave a hundred per-cent, I never gave up, that was the way I had been brought up. From the age of about nine I used to have to work in the Cattle Market with all my family on Saturday mornings, and after washing down all the cows and rubbing them down with sawdust, all the men and boys used to have a big football match. They were real battles, hard, dirty and bruising, but as a kid you learned to look after yourself and toughen up, which I expect prepared me for my life as a professional footballer. These ding-dong games used to go on for an hour while the cattle dried and I remember being sent crashing into big, iron cattle-pens - my uncles simply told me to get up and get on with the game. When I arrived at Chelsea I was tough enough.

My relationship with the crowd is something I was proud of and there was a good turn-out, 17,000, for my testimonial, which was fantastic for a Monday night game. Jimmy Greaves once said that as a footballer, "I had a heart the size of a cabbage". That one quote still means more than anything else that has even been written about me.

Up front was Roy Bentley, our hard-as-nails centre-forward and inspirational captain. Roy was a fantastic finisher, had a great shot and was so strong in the air. Few people realise how tough he was. I remember playing up at Hartlepools in the FA Cup and their full-backs kicked myself and Eric Parsons off the park. Harlepools had a kid of a right-back who had kicked the most lumps out of me, but he made the mistake of then turning his attention to Roy and started to kick him too. At one stage he grabbed Roy by the throat and started to threaten him, the next thing we knew the Harlepools defender was spark out, unconscious on the ground with two of his front teeth missing. The really funny thing about that incident is that the following week, the Hartlepools manager, Fred Westgarth, sent Chelsea a dental bill for two false teeth. The referee saw what happened, he watched Roy head-butt the defender, but he didn't send him off, you never got sent off back then. The lad asked for it though and the referee was probably quite pleased that somebody had sorted out the nasty piece of work. In those days it was a different game, that's how justice was meted out, it wasn't every man for himself but it was a far harder game. I wouldn't say it was a dirtier game, but it was certainly a more physical contest.

Mind you, when we played Newcastle at St. James' Park during the Championship campaign we came up against a Scotsman called Jimmy Scoular, now he *was* a dirty so-and-so. I remember kicking him by accident and him getting up and telling me that he would get me back later. In the second half the ball was knocked out for a throw-in over on my flank and I knew that Derek Saunders was going to throw it towards me, so I kept shaking my head and trying to tell him not to. It was clear that Scoular was standing right behind me and I could sense this was payback time. Despite making it obvious I didn't want the ball anywhere near me, the silly bugger threw it straight to my feet and I was immediately kicked up into the air and the trainer had to come on to treat me for quite a while. Five minutes or so after that Scoular came running alongside me and said; "alright Frank, that's one each, shall we call it quits now?" As quick as a flash I replied, "yep, that'll do me Jimmy!" And that was the end of it, thank God!

Another striker who played a significant part in our success was Seamus O'Connell, who was a cattle farmer in Carlisle during the week. But we never saw him from match to match, and despite scoring eight goals in eleven matches that year he only played the one season for Chelsea. He was a good little player who I'd compare to Jimmy Greaves in some respects because he had the knack of being in the right place at the right time. To give him credit he was a good finisher, either in the air or shooting and I would say that seventy-five percent of his attempts were on target, which says a lot. But none of the players ever got to know him too well because he never trained with us and disappeared straight after matches to catch the train back to Carlisle. We'd see him in the changing room for an hour before the game, then as soon as he was bathed and changed, he was gone again. He never knew us and we never knew him and Seamus has never been at any of our team's re-unions.

During the Championship season Chelsea set up an exhibition game against the Hungarian Champions, Red Banner and 40,000 fans turned up on a Wednesday afternoon to see the game - everyone must have skipped off work. Red Banner were made up largely of the Hungarian international side that had famously thrashed England six-three at Wembley, so it was a bit of a grudge game and we certainly wanted to beat them. They were a really good side but we should have won. Chelsea missed two penalties and the game ended two-all.

I think it was purely coincidental that Chelsea won their first and only top flight Championship in their Golden Jubilee season, I can't recall anyone mentioning the fiftieth anniversary to the players until after the season and there were certainly no celebrations to mark the occasion apart from the players' achievement. We were just concentrating on one game at a time, picking up the points and getting our £2 win bonuses. Afterwards, though, a lot of the journalists were making a big thing of both landmarks arriving at the same time, and I notice that there's talk among them again predicting Chelsea will win The Premier League in 2005 because that is the club's centenary. But I'm not so sure.

After clinching the title following the 3-0 home win against Sheffield Wednesday in the penultimate game of the season, all the players were called back into the Directors' Box to salute the crowd, which was brilliant. But I still don't think we realised what we'd achieved. It shows how difficult it is to win the title, because Chelsea have failed to win it since. There was no trophy at the ground or anything and we certainly never ran around the pitch. Our reward for winning the title? We had the option of choosing between £20 or two suits from a shop called Pollicoffs in the East End of London! We didn't even go out after the game, there was no party and I think I had a sandwich and a cup of tea in the boardroom before coming straight home. It'd be all champagne and fireworks now.

Within six years Chelsea were relegated though, from the top to the bottom of the First Division. Ted Drake let too many of the experienced lads go too quickly in my opinion, Drake's Ducklings his team became known as. It's all very well bringing kids into the side, but we didn't have enough experience alongside them. Two or three youngsters are fine, the team can carry those, but when you have six or seven to look after it becomes really hard work and from being the youngest in the side when I joined, I became the eldest. Don't get me wrong, some of the young players were brilliant, Jimmy Greaves, Ken Shellito, Peter Bonetti, Terry Venables, etc., but there were too many changes, and on reflection, Chelsea would have fared better if the transition had been made more slowly.

But over all I had fifteen great years at Chelsea and I am proud to have been part of that team. We were good ambassadors for the club I think, none of us ever caused any trouble and we can feel honoured that we are still the only players to have won a top flight Championship at Stamford Bridge.

Chelsea were a great club to us too, it was reciprocal, but Chelsea is a different club today to the one I was at and our achievements aren't recognised any more for some reason. Some people have recently insinuated that we weren't a good team, but it's the only real Championship Chelsea have ever won. I know the die-hard supporters of the club appreciate us, the reception we received when we went onto the pitch a few seasons ago proved that and it brought tears to my eyes. I know the people that really matter, the fans, don't want to brush me and my team-mates under the carpet. Whatever our detractors think, we achieved something special for a fantastic club and some fantastic supporters; other football clubs are proud of what past generations have achieved and Chelsea should be equally proud of its heritage in my opinion.

When I went back for the first time since Stamford Bridge's redesign I look around the new stadium and tried visualising the place as it was when I played, trying to picture the Shed, the 'new' stand and a packed bowl of terracing, but it was almost impossible. So much has changed.

Stan
Willemse

As a kid I played for Brighton Boys, Sussex Boys and England Boys, winning more or less every prize a kid could get back then, but I became a professional footballer through a strange series of events. At the age of fourteen I started work as a labourer, but I got sacked because I put my foot through a ceiling, that was just before the War broke out, so I decided to join up as a Royal Marine Commando and served in France. Brighton had obviously already spotted me at that stage.

I played for The Albion on and off as a guest during wartime on an amateur basis when I came home on leave, so when I was de-mobbed in 1946, I signed professional with The Seagulls for £5 a week. I started to play well, so went and asked for a rise. Charlie Webb was manager then and he bumped me up to £8 a week at the end of that first season, that was really good money in 1947. I then had a big setback to my career because I was told I had to have a mastoid operation, which was a very big thing to have done in those days. The surgeons told me that after they'd opened my head up I would probably never play football again, but believe it or not I was back playing in the first team within six weeks. That wasn't going to beat me.

Don Welsh took over as manager at The Goldstone soon afterwards and one day he called me into his office and said he wanted to sell me. Back then you didn't have a choice, you had to go where you were told really, so I asked him where I was off to. He said there were several clubs in for me - Southampton, Sheffield United and Chelsea. I had such a limited knowledge of football outside Brighton, I was born and bred in the town and I still live there today. I had to get the manager to tell me about the three different clubs, where they were and if they were any good. I also had a wife and kids to think about, so when the manager told me that Chelsea was just outside Victoria Station and I probably wouldn't have to move away from Brighton, I decided to come up to Stamford Bridge and speak with Bill Birrell the manager.

I made my way up to London and had a good chat with Mr. Birrell, who told me he needed some new faces in his defence and wanted to buy me to play as an understudy to left-back Bill Hughes, who was a Welsh international, but was getting on a bit. I told the Chelsea manager that I would be happy to sign even though he'd warned me I may not be in the first team for quite a while. My wages went up to £11 and the club also paid my travelling expenses to and from Brighton every day, so at £6000, I became Brighton's record transfer. My signing-on fee was a whopping £10 and I even had to fight to get that!

I joined up with the squad for pre-season training at the start of the 1949-50 season and played my first game for the reserves on the opening day. After just a handful of games Mr. Birrell called me into his office and asked me if I wanted to play in the first team against Arsenal; was I up to it? Billy Hughes had got injured against Derby a couple of days earlier, so I told him that I'd love to be given the chance, of course I was up to the challenge. So lo and behold I got my chance almost straight away and on my Chelsea debut we beat The Gunners three-two at Highbury on a Wednesday evening. When we came into training the next day the manager called me to one side and told me that he was very happy with the way I'd played and he thought I'd done well, which I suppose I had because not many of the Arsenal lads got past me.

I was in and out of the side for most of that season, Bill Hughes, Sid Bathgate and myself used to vie for the same position, but at the end of the season Birrell got sacked and Hughes moved to non-league Hereford United. When Ted Drake arrived I became the natural successor to the left-back berth and my career at Chelsea really took off. I played over two hundred and twenty games for the club in a little over five years and I was hardly ever out injured. I remember one of the few times I did become ill was during the Championship season and Ted sent me and the missus away to Folkestone for the weekend to recuperate which was good of him. But a few days later he rang me up to make sure I hadn't been relaxing too much as he wanted to recall me at outside-left, so I didn't get much rest! Frank Blunstone was missing with the England squad for their game against Scotland and he wanted to play me out on the flank against Sunderland. I'd played in that position as a kid, but never as a professional, but I couldn't have done badly because I scored the winning goal against Sunderland with my weaker, right foot. Ted decided to keep me there for the next game too, away at Tottenham and we won 4-2.

Commuting to and from the South Coast was always great fun as Eric Parsons, John McNichol and a big reserve centre-forward called Ernie Randall all caught the train up together. We caught the 8.30am train up to Victoria every morning and would finish training by midday and all get the train back again about 1pm. We played a lot of cards on the train and used to win a few quid off each other, but nothing silly. Quite often, because the club gave us free tickets for the theatre or the cinema, plus I had a free season ticket on the trains, me and the wife would come straight back up to the London Palladium in the evening for a night out.

The trains didn't always work in our favour though, I remember one Boxing Day we played Portsmouth at Fratton Park. It was a late morning kick-off, so we asked at the station what time the trains back to Brighton ran so the three of us could get back home as quickly as possible after the game. We were told the best train to catch would be at 3.20pm, so all the Chelsea boys got on the coach back to London while the Brighton clan stayed behind at the ground for a couple of drinks because we had a bit of time to kill. We got to the station in plenty of time, or so we thought, only to be told by the Station Master that we'd missed the Brighton train by twenty minutes and there wasn't another one for over two hours. What a miserable Christmas that was, there were no cafés open, no pubs, nothing.

The social scene was quite good, Ted Drake liked his golf and his horse racing and he used to take us out. I remember Ted took us racing to Chantilly when we were over in France for a post-season tour after the Championship season and we were talking to some of the trainers asking for tips and advice. One of them told me to back his horse for The English Derby the following week, saying; "my horse will win and it has a name like your manager - Phil Drake". I turned round to Ted and laughed, "will you remember that Guv'nor?" I said. Lo and behold the horse only won! I had followed the French owner's advice and made about £300, but when I asked Ted how much he'd won he told me he'd backed something else because he'd forgotten the name of the horse! Ted was always nice to me, we never fell out and he was a gentleman as far as I was concerned. His only fault from my perspective was that I didn't feel he was very good at coaching, but I guess in those days not many managers had realised how important that aspect of the game was. Billy Birrell, Ted's predecessor, just used to sit in his office all day and we never saw him on the training pitch from one week to the next, but Ted was far more involved than him.

The only time I really remember Ted losing his temper badly was when we played Cardiff at Ninian Park on Boxing Day 1955. We travelled down to Wales on the train on Christmas Day afternoon and got to our hotel some time in the evening. Ted told us all to get something to eat, have a quick drink, then get ourselves to bed early. The Guv'nor thought we should get our heads down at a reasonable hour because the kick-off against Cardiff was at 11.30 the following morning. Most of the players did as he asked, but a few of us older ones gave each other a sly look when he was talking and I knew a few of the lads would be up for a little Christmas drink-up in one of the player's rooms. So we ordered some crates of Brown Ale up to my room and Johnny McNichol, Roy Bentley, Peter Sillett and myself were having a great time. Then all of a sudden, about one o'clock in the morning, there was a very loud knock on the door. When we opened up there stood Ted Drake and he absolutely blew his nut! I said, "Guv'nor, don't lose your rag, we'd beat Cardiff tomorrow even if we stayed up drinking all night!" He didn't see the funny side

1954 – Stan Willemse swings his trusty left foot to clear the ball

April 1955 – Chelsea go close against Tottenham in the 4-2 win at White Hart Lane

October 1954 — Ken Armstrong in action during Chelsea's 1-0 defeat at Blackpool

of it at all and ushered us all straight to bed with the warning that he'd deal with us all in the morning. We drew one-all but beat them two-one at Stamford Bridge twenty-four hours later.

Ted had set his eyes on the Cup rather than the League before the Championship season started I think, he even admitted that during his speech on the balcony at Stamford Bridge after we'd clinched the title against Sheffield Wednesday, but he was so proud to have won something so significant for Chelsea and the players worked so hard all season long.

When we went up to the outfitters to claim our Championship prizes, a suit, I spotted a Crombie overcoat, which were all the rage at the time, so I ordered one of those as well! At the start of the next season Ted called me into his office and said to me, "Stan, you had a heavy bill at the tailors, how come yours was twice as much as everyone else's?" I had to laugh, I told him that I'd got the coat too - he just smiled back and waved me out of his office. I think he knew I deserved it!

I only missed a handful of games during the Championship season and made the left-back position my own. In my opinion Chelsea had a great defence and I was proud to be part of it. We were all big lads, good in the air with two great little wing-halves in front of us in Ken Armstrong [pictured left] and Derek Saunders. Ken Armstrong was one of the finest footballers I ever played with and boy did he love a game of cards! One day he turned up at training with a new car, he was the first player at Chelsea to own one. As he got out a few of us said, "how did you afford that Kenny?" He just smiled back and replied, "thanks lads, I bought this from my winnings off you lot this season!" My first car was an old hearse!

Ken would run for ninety minutes, his passing was so precise and when he had to, he got stuck in too. You could tell Kenny enjoyed playing the game just by watching him, but then again, we all did! Ken moved to New Zealand in the end and that's where he died unfortunately. Derek Saunders, who was an amateur when he arrived at Stamford Bridge, but went on to become an excellent professional too.

Stan Wicks was another fantastic player in the centre of our defence and I always felt more comfortable once Wicksy had taken the place of Ron Greenwood. Ron was an excellent player, but he was a ball-player and liked to pass out of defence, which I always thought was a 'no-no'. I just got rid of the ball otherwise I knew I'd find myself back in trouble sooner or later. Stan Wicks had the same outlook, he was a lovely lad.

I always felt a bit sorry for some of the reserves in our squad because a lot of them were very good players, but they only got their chance when people got injured. During the Championship season we didn't suffer too much from important players getting crocked so there must have been some very frustrated players who never quite got their chance to shine at Stamford Bridge. Over all, though, I found the Championship season just as exciting as my other seasons at Chelsea, in my eyes things only really got hot during the run-in. But I will always remember the fans running onto the pitch at the final whistle when we'd clinched it. There must have been 40,000 people on the grass at Stamford Bridge, they all jumped over the dog track and over to the players. I was shaking people's hands for a good twenty minutes before making my way to get changed. It was such a low-key celebration that I caught the train home at the normal time and I went racing at Brighton to see my dogs running. The trip to Victoria Station on the tube was special though, with all the fans coming up to me and patting me on the back.

It was disappointing not to make the full England team while I was at Chelsea like some of the other lads had, but I was up against some very good and established players at the time and selection always seemed to favour the regulars. I was called up for the 'B' side, England manager Walter Winterbottom took a team out to Bulgaria and told myself and Manchester United's Roger Byrne that whoever had the best games on the tour would win a regular place in the side. To be fair I didn't play well and missed out over the next three years. I was always in contention for a place and was selected for FA representative games, but I never managed to get a full cap, which is a regret. Because of that trip to Eastern Europe I also missed Chelsea's tour to New York and Canada, which I was just as gutted about.

I wasn't a classy player, but I thought I stuck to my defensive task well and I had a presence on the pitch, the opponents certainly knew I was playing and I had a reputation. I could pass a ball, my game wasn't all about intimidation, but you were allowed to tackle from behind in that era and shoulder barging was acceptable too, so I used to enjoy my games. I'm so pleased that referees allowed the game to flow and I played in an era when bookings and sendings off were almost unheard of. I don't think I would have stayed on the pitch five minutes otherwise.

Referees used to speak to you and tick you off, but that was about it. I remember one coming over to me after I'd caught a player late and he just said, "I wondered when you were going to get him with a good'un, that winger has been taking the piss out of you all afternoon!" Another time, away at Charlton in our 2-0 win in 1955, I'd taken their winger out twice and the crowd were all on my back, booing and calling me all the names under the sun. So the referee came walking over to me wagging his finger, pretending to the supporters that he was ticking me off. But all he said to me was, "now, now Stan... Are you going to the races on

1955 – Stan Willemse sucks on a half time lemon during a friendly with Hayes Town

Monday?" I looked at the ground, as if I was sorry, then replied, "yeah, I'll be there ref..." "Cut that out and I'll see you at the first race..." he said, then blew his whistle for the free kick to be taken.

I had right battles with some players during games, but as soon as the match was over, that was the end of it, I can't remember having a running feud with anyone. I had some good scraps with a player called Trevor Ford, he was at Sunderland and Cardiff - he was one of the hardest centre-forwards in the game. You could hit him, kick him, swear at him, rub mud in his face when he was on the ground, anything, but he'd just give as good as he got and we'd walk off the pitch arm in arm. Another time Arsenal came to The Bridge and a week before the game everyone was talking about Danny Clapton and myself coming head-to-head, but during the game we just 'hand-bagged it'. I think we left the crowd a bit disappointed you know. Every time he got the ball he passed it, every time I got the ball I got rid of it, we spent most of the match keeping out of each other's way. So I didn't go looking for trouble for the sake of it, well, not every week.

We used to know referees by their first names, and if you did something genuinely serious they could send you off, but they just let the game flow. I think the only player I saw sent off in the whole time I was at Chelsea was our inside-forward Jimmy Bowie, and that was only because he called the referee something a little too strong for his own good. I was supposed to be a hard man, but I was never booked in my whole career, so I must have been angelic really!

Tom Finney once wrote in a newspaper interview that I was the hardest defender in the game, but he also said that he always admired me because I was fair. The next time we came face to face on the pitch I said to him "alright Tom, thanks..." and smiled, but I don't think I was any less hard or any fairer with him during the match itself!

The most exciting game of the Championship season, apart from the games that actually clinched our crown at the end, was the five-six defeat at The Bridge to Manchester United. Our defence had an absolute stinker that day, but so did their's to be fair and the spectators must have loved the match. Chelsea supporters were very cosmopolitan, they wanted to see a good game. They would obviously prefer it if Chelsea won, but the home fans would often clap and cheer if the opposition scored a good goal or there was an individual piece of skill by the other side. I get the impression today that the home fans want to win at all cost and are far more partisan. In the home game against Preston that season Tom Finney was making a monkey out of me and the Chelsea fans were cheering him! But on the whole I had a lovely relationship with the supporters, especially the ones in the Shed, they were my pride and joy.

1955 — Stan Willemse [second from right] and the lads share a joke during training

If you stayed at a club for five years, it was in your contract that you were entitled to a benefit payment. Because wages weren't particularly high in those days, players depended on the windfall, and mine was due in the Championship season. One day in training I was running round the edge of the pitch and Mr. Pratt, one of the Directors, called me over. I remember thinking how unusual it was to see someone from the Board out for training. When I went over he handed me a cheque for £750, which was a lot of money - he told me to take it straight to the bank. The tax man had to take his cut, but I must be fair to Chelsea, as soon as it was due, it was paid. It doesn't seem right that today, when a player gets a testimonial, they're allowed to keep every penny and not pay tax, even when they earn a fortune.

Because of the amount of younger players that Ted Drake had successfully brought in to help us win the title, The Guv'nor thought he could do away with the majority of the older boys and bring in more and more kids, which was his downfall in the end. Unfortunately he got rid of too many, too soon. There was no ill-feeling, he let go of people as nicely as he could, including myself, but he should have done it over a longer period. Within twelve months of winning the title Ted had transformed the side.

After Chelsea I moved to Leyton Orient who were managed by Alec Stock, but what a disaster that turned out to be. Because I didn't want to travel to East London every day, Alec said I could train down in Brighton, but it wasn't the same just running round the park on my own and my fitness went downhill at a frightening rate. Within a year wingers were skipping by me, at Chelsea a winger would never intentionally get past! I couldn't believe it when Orient drew Chelsea in the F.A. Cup the year I moved to Brisbane Road.

Peter Brabrook, who was still only a boy really, was outside-right for Chelsea that day and I was marking him. I didn't care how old he was though, I made sure I played my usual no-nonsense game and was as determined as ever that the forward wasn't going to get the better of me. After the game I remember Ted Drake coming to find me and having a word in my ear about being too hard. He said to me, "Stan, I didn't think you'd play like that against Peter..." I just replied, "well that's the way you expected me to play last season when I was at Chelsea!"

I'll never forget the last game of the Championship season up at Old Trafford, all the United players had lined up and clapped us as we ran out onto the pitch. That was a fantastic gesture I thought, we were very honoured that such a good side had given us that kind of respect, although I was pleased when the referee blew his whistle for the start of the game so we could go back to hating them again! They beat us

2-1 and were the only side in the division to do the double over Chelsea that season.

I loved the times that I've been back to the club over the years, it's always great to sit down with the fans and reminisce. I've been in the bar at Stamford Bridge until the early hours just talking to supporters I've never met before about playing for the club, I enjoyed every minute of it. I hope that Chelsea do win the Premier League soon, that way the burden will be off our shoulders, I know that the club would dearly love to win something again and I wish them well.

John
Harris

September 1954 — John Harris during Chelsea's 2-1 win at Sheffield United

November 1954 — John Harris warms up before Chelsea's 1-1 draw at Sheffield Wednesday

John had an early moment of glory with Chelsea, Captaining the team that won the League South Cup against Millwall at Wembley in 1945. He originally joined the club on loan from Wolves during The War and Billy Birrell signed him permanently as soon as the fighting was over. John was a tremendous centre-half for Chelsea, not only the kingpin of the side but a great Captain until Roy Bentley took over as skipper.

In my opinion John's finest match for Chelsea was against Sunderland at Stamford Bridge in 1950 when he marked Trevor Ford out of the match. Ford had been due to sign for Chelsea from Aston Villa, but at the eleventh hour Sunderland grabbed him which was a big blow for the club. By coincidence Ford's debut was at The Bridge the next day and the crowd gave him a hostile reception. John Harris seemed to make it a personal challenge that Ford would stay in his pocket the whole game and Chelsea won three-nil.

John was a hard man who could mix it with the best, but he could play a bit too and that should not be forgotten. John went on to manage Chester and Sheffield United after leaving Stamford Bridge but Chelsea was always in his heart from the time he joined the club during the war until he died in 1988. *Albert Sewell*

John
McNichol

Early on in my career I played for local sides around Kilmarnock in Scotland, but I had a job in a shop so I didn't really play much competitive football for about eighteen months. Eventually I played for a side called Hurlford Juniors, who were a semi-professional team and well worth playing for in my situation because I'd become an apprentice motor mechanic by that time. When you were only earning nine or ten shillings a week as a trainee in a garage, to earn another five shillings through playing football on a Saturday afternoon was heaven. I played there until I got called up to the Fleet Air Arm during the War, then all my football games were mostly played for fun.

Because I was stationed in the north of Scotland I turned out for a Highlands League side called Clachnacuddin a few times, and because I took the game so seriously, I was recommended to a few Football League sides in England. When I was de-mobbed I was invited down to Huddersfield, who were supposed to be interested in me, but that turned out to be a real waste of time. So I came back to Scotland thinking I'd sign for Kilmarnock.

Before I'd had a chance to sign for The Killies I was told that Newcastle United wanted to take a look at me, news which I was obviously very interested in. So I travelled down for a trial and was invited to take part in a pre-season First Team v Second Team match. I couldn't believe that so many fans turned up to watch – the supporters were so passionate up there that even games like that sold out. I had a good match and the manager, Stan Seymour, came over and said he wanted to speak to me in his office. I hadn't intended to sign for them straight away, even though they were such a big club, so when he offered me the terms and conditions of a contract there and then, I told him that I'd have to go back to Scotland and sort a few things out. He was shocked, his eyes almost popped out of his head, he thought I was stalling on signing. I quickly reassured him that I wanted to sign but I had to go and sort my job out. He was really understanding and said he definitely wanted me and asked me back the following week for another match.

I returned seven days later and signed, but I asked him if it was okay just to play part time, as I wanted to finish my apprenticeship. Newcastle was such a rich side at the time, they were signing players left, right and centre, so the manager wasn't too concerned about my request because he didn't expect me to be in the first team for a while. At that stage Newcastle had possibly the greatest striking line-up of all time, Jackie Milburn, Len Shackleton, Charlie Wayman and Roy Bentley.

To continue my apprenticeship I got a job in an undertakers very close to St. James' Park, which had half a dozen Rolls Royces for me to look after. The fella who owned the undertakers was also a big Newcastle fan, so I was getting £5 per week at the undertakers and £6 per week from Newcastle United. I was earning the same kind of wages as top players, so the situation couldn't really have been much better. I don't think I trained during the day more than six times in the two years I was at Newcastle, all my training was done in the evening, but there were other players doing the same as me, so I wasn't unique. This arrangement went on for two seasons and in that time Newcastle got promoted back to Division One, following relegation before the War.

Eventually I was called back in to see the manager who told me he wanted me to go full time for £10 a week. But that didn't make sense to me, I was earning more as things stood so I was reluctant to agree. I had a good friend at Newcastle called Norman Dodgin, a right-half who had just got into the first team, his brother Bill was the manager of Southampton. Norman said that his brother was interested in signing me, but at the same time I was told that Brighton's Don Welsh had also been onto Newcastle about buying me. Brighton said they'd offer me top wages of £12, whether I was in the first team or not, which was a fantastic deal. So I moved all the way from Newcastle to Brighton.

I did well on the South Coast, playing for The Seagulls really put me in the shop window and it wasn't too long before bigger clubs were interested in me again. Manchester City came in with a good offer, but I'd only been at Brighton for a short while and they couldn't guarantee me first team football at Maine Road, or any more money because of the maximum wage rules, so I stayed put. Ted Drake must have first noticed me when I played for Brighton at Reading - he was manager at Elm Park at the time. We beat them four-one and I scored a second half hat-trick. I must have annoyed and impressed him at the same time because when he joined Chelsea at the start of the 1952-53 season, I became his first signing. [See picture on page 73]

Chelsea were obviously a class above Brighton and Ted Drake seemed a very nice fella - honest and easy going. Getting into the first team straight away was good for me too although we didn't do well that first season. Chelsea struggled against relegation and only stayed up on goal average in the end. We were in the relegation zone until the last game of the season before beating Manchester City 3-1 at Stamford Bridge. They went down instead of us.

In 1953-54 we finshed eighth and had a far better campaign. Ted had started to make his mark at the club and his vision of winning the League within three years was starting to take shape. Chelsea had a very big squad of players in those days, there must have been something like sixty players on the club's books and there were four teams. With the kind of crowds that the club were bringing in, plus the maximum wage limiting the wage expenditure, it must have been more affordable to have big squads of players. But some days it was so crammed there were no pegs remaining to hang your coat on. Training was basic though.

I remember running down the Embankment and through the streets with the squad during pre-season training in the sunshine, it was a lovely route. We used to go over Chelsea Bridge and through Battersea Park, which had housed The British Exhibition since just after The War. We did most of our training on the Stamford Bridge pitch though, so you can imagine what sort of state that used to be in as the season wore on. Ted Drake took us to Broadstairs in Kent three times during the Championship season, to relax, play a bit of golf and to bond the team further. I got the feeling that Ted was a superstitious man, we'd been there before and results improved afterwards, so he thought Broadstairs was lucky. None of the players were superstitious though, apart from those who thought it was lucky to stand outside the changing room having a smoke ten minutes before the game and during half time!

There was no doubt that Ted Drake was a gentleman and a fantastic player in his day, but I'd taken coaching courses before I'd arrived at Chelsea and I think I knew ten times more than he did about structuring training sessions. Ted was a 'get stuck in' sort of character who enjoyed the blood and thunder atmosphere of the match rather than intricate training exercises.

My first game for Chelsea was against the Champions, Manchester United away, on August 23rd, 1952. I remember our right-back, Sid Bathgate, got injured and I had to go back into defence and cover. I was marking a player called Roger Byrne, who was an Old Trafford and England regular for years, so to be playing out of position in such an important game made for an eventful debut. We lost two-nil on the opening day of the 1952-53 season, but little did I know then that under two years later we'd emerge as the title winners ourselves.

The game that I think changed us from contenders into Champions elect was the match at White Hart Lane against Spurs in early April '55. We won four-two, coming from behind twice, but the victory was even more impressive because we were missing Frank Blunstone and Ken Armstrong who were away on international duty for the England-Scotland international. I scored two goals that day, Stan Wicks got a header and Peter Sillett scored from a penalty, but I also remember that Stan Willemse was spat at when he ran out of the tunnel - the Spurs fans didn't like Stan! To win that away game at Spurs gave us a huge lift and put us four points clear at the top, but Wolves had two games in hand on us, with Portsmouth, Manchester United and Manchester City not far

1952 – John McNichol signs his new contract to become Ted Drake's first signing

April 1955 — Sheffield Wednesday's goalie congratulates John after 3-0 win at The Bridge

behind. The league was so tight, nobody had ever edged ahead, not by more than a few points, so it was always critical not to lose those kinds of games, as it would allow your rivals to make up ground.

With Wolves breathing down our necks, doing the double over them was clearly vital and I'm sure when we won at their place it damaged their belief. I remember as the players were walking off the pitch after winning at Molineux one of their lads walked over to shake my hand and said that his team were going to get murdered by their manager for losing to Chelsea, he was genuinely worried about Stan Cullis' reaction. Wolves had been in control for a lot of the game but we never gave up and to win 4-3 up there was tremendous.

I scored forty-three goals for Chelsea, including fourteen during the Championship season, but the strangest goal I had a part in that year was against Leicester in a three-one win at The Bridge just before Christmas '54. I hit the ball well which beat the 'keeper, only for it to hit the underside of the bar and bounce on the goal line. The two full-backs, Froggatt and Milburn, were so confused about what to do with the ball that they both kicked it at exactly the same time and it went straight into the back of the net. That is the only time I can remember one own goal being credited to two separate players! I was a bit disappointed that they'd made contact really as the ball was going to roll back into the net and would have been my goal, but it was a real catalogue of errors and very funny to watch from a supporter's point of view.

The biggest problem with Chelsea's Championship win, and the main reason that so little is really known about it, is the fact that there was a national newspaper strike on for a large part of the season, so our achievements weren't being reported. The week when we clinched the title only a handful of reports were published so the event was a bit of a flounce. Even when the newspapers were being printed, very few of them were saying complimentary things about us, they were very unimpressed with Chelsea. I don't know what rubbed them up the wrong way about us, we were an attractive side and our games were always exciting, but I got the impression that the only people who were genuinely pleased that we won the title were our own supporters. Wolverhampton Wanderers and Manchester United, who won the titles before and after Chelsea, were treated in a far more complimentary fashion.

It was a very open division, even until the final few weeks any one of up to five clubs were still in with a shout of glory, but that was the case most seasons, unlike today when the same two clubs have a monopoly on things. More or less any club was capable of topping the league because they all had the same sized squads, every player earned the same amount of money and the win bonuses were equal no matter where you played. It made for a more even competition and right until the final weeks of most seasons, you really had no idea who would clinch the honours.

After the home win against Sheffield Wednesday I remember looking down at all the thousands of fans on the pitch and all the players being introduced to the fans accompanied by huge cheers. The celebrations were short-lived, when that was over five of us just went to the café round the corner for a cup of tea and some chips - which makes me laugh when I look back. That was our big celebration night, a cuppa, a chip butty and an early night!

Roy Bentley was probably the best player in the side and deserved to be Captain. Because he was a centre-forward it was sometimes difficult for him to lead from that position, but he dropped back and covered a lot which meant he was still able to communicate with the rest of the side. The role of Captain hadn't developed as it has in the modern game, but Roy would never expect you to do anything he wasn't prepared to do himself and was a fine leader for Chelsea. Roy was always on the run, he never stopped moving, trying to find a good position, and speaking as a winger, he was the perfect player to deliver a cross to because he was so strong in the air. I'd say that 90% of the time he would win the ball, no matter who the defender was. With Roy in the side you could be more direct when you needed to be. Peter Sillett had a terrific kick on him and if we were chasing a game, when time was running out, we could launch a ball into the area knowing there was a good chance that Roy could nod it down for somebody else. He was definitely a good player to have on your side. Roy wasn't half the player at Newcastle that he became at Chelsea, but at The Magpies he wasn't as strong and I'm not sure he was too well. Being at Stamford Bridge certainly brought the best out in him.

It was a tough old game for an inside-forward like myself and I had my cheek bone fractured three times while I was playing, only once at Chelsea, but all were sustained going up for headers. If you got kicked, you just got up, because if a player rolled around and made the most of it, players from both sides would shout at them to get on with it. There's a hell of a lot of cheating that goes on today that didn't exist in our time, but I look at the game these days and realise I would have got more protection as a forward.

Ted and I fell out slightly when I bought a newsagents shop in Brighton, but I was almost thirty-two at that stage and I had to start thinking of my life after football. Most of the other older players from the Championship side had moved on or retired from the game by then, so I knew it was only a matter of time before I had to make way too.

Looking back, I guess he may have had a point about my shop, it did involve me getting up at six in the morning, sorting out all the papers for the paperboys, then rushing to catch the 8.15 train to London – my goal-scoring went right off the boil.

I eventually had to make way at Chelsea for a young player you may have heard of by the name of Jimmy Greaves, who had cleaned my boots before then. Jimmy was a paperboy too when he first started at Chelsea, and because he knew I ran a newsagents, he told me about all the pranks he used to get up to on his morning rounds.

I moved on to Crystal Palace after Chelsea and had some good years there, then I went into management with Tunbridge Wells, before going back to Selhurst Park to look after their lottery and fund raising for about eleven years. I then moved almost full circle returning to Brighton and Hove Albion until I retired from a similar role. Luckily I was involved in the game from 1946 all the way up until 1992 in one way or another.

Ken
Armstrong

Champion team-mates Ken Armstrong [left] & Eric Parsons share a bath at The Bridge

1958 — Ken Armstrong and his family emigrate to New Zealand

1955 – Roy Bentley and Ken Armstrong before an 8-0 friendly win at Hayes

Ken was an important signing by Billy Birrell just after the War. Chelsea needed a right-half, but more importantly at the time, the team needed a stop-gap centre-forward to replace Tommy Lawton, who was a big loss to the club and especially the fans. So for a time Ken was played out of position, but he was the kind of guy who would play anywhere he was asked.

When Roy Bentley arrived from Newcastle Ken moved back to his more accustomed place at right-half and turned into one of the best wing-halves that Chelsea has ever had. He was always so dependable, so fit and consistent.

In 1958 Ken decided to emigrate to New Zealand with his family and became an important man in the New Zealand Football Association, but sadly he died there in 1984. Ken was a pivotal part of Chelsea's Championship win. *Albert Sewell*

Roy
Bentley

I left school in 1938 at the age of fourteen and signed for Bristol Rovers as a ground-staff boy. The wages were £1 per week and we really had to work hard for that. There was no coaching or training provided during the day, I just worked on the ground and stadium - so it seemed that I was more of an odd-job boy than a football trainee. Sometimes we went back after work to play football in the evenings, but I learned more about building and DIY to be honest.

Joe Davis, a famous Snooker player of the time, was a Director at Rovers and almost single handedly keeping the club alive through his donations. Rovers were in big financial trouble and were on the verge of going out of business. One of the cuts the club imposed was reducing the pay of all the players, everyone was told they had to take a pay cut and mine were reduced to just 10 shillings a week. That wasn't enough for me to live on, so my Dad told me that I should leave and join Bristol City, who also wanted me, so I followed his advice. It was far better at Ashton Gate, even though I continued doing lots of work around the stadium. As well as the odd-jobs, I also looked after the club's horse and rolled the pitch. But within a very short time The War had started and things began to change very quickly for me.

A lot of the City players were called up to join the Forces which led to me being drafted into the first team, the club were struggling to field a side and I seized the opportunity. The change in circumstances meant that I was now being provided with the best possible training a young player could get. During The War a lot of international players guested for Bristol City, so as a sixteen-year-old kid playing out on the wing, I had all their experience and knowledge to feed from. There were some great players passing through the club. City were eventually paying them £5 a game, which attracted England internationals like George Tadman, Eddie Hapgood and Ron Dicks to Ashton Gate.

I learned the tricks of the trade by working with those kind of players, but it was Billy Mitchell in particular, a wing-half who played for Chelsea and Ireland in the early 1930s, who had the biggest influence on me at the time. Billy used to give me half an hour at the end of every training session dedicated to looking after myself on the football pitch. I've never passed on anything that Billy told me to any other player and his lessons contributed a big part in helping me to the top in football. He taught me a few little tricks, 'subtle' tools of the trade that referees would never see, lessons that gave me a big advantage over any opponent. By the looks of it Alan Shearer has had a few lessons from old Billy too.

At the same time Billy instilled some less rudimentary principles and taught me how I should conduct myself on the field and how to behave if I wanted to become a top player. Billy told me that if he ever caught me putting in an intentionally-late tackle on somebody, he'd do the same to me in training. He encouraged me to be the best I possibly could and to believe in my ability. His experience showed me how to use my strengths on the pitch as well as how to protect myself if I had to, but my Dad had been a bare-knuckle fist fighter, so I think I already had an understanding of how to look after myself if need be!

Because of my age and the continuing War, Bristol City were concerned that they would lose me when my time came to join the Navy, so I was offered a professional contract just before my seventeenth birthday. The last game I played before I was due to set sail was against Cardiff City. What rough old games they always were! Most of the Cardiff lads were miners and loved a good scrap, and during the game, one of them threatened that if I went past him down the wing one more time, he'd break my legs. I wasn't going to be intimidated, so I skipped past him some more to prove the point. Just before half time, though, he clattered into me and broke my ankle. I didn't know the extent of the injury at the time and still managed to take my girlfriend (now my wife of fifty-seven years) out dancing that night as it was our last night together, but I couldn't put any weight on it and the swelling was so bad I had to be taken to the hospital first thing the next morning. I was due to sail the following day, but the doctors told me I couldn't possibly leave and I would have to miss my ship. In a strange twist of fate, the ship was attacked during the journey I should have been on, and although I didn't know it at the time, that tackle almost certainly saved my life.

While I was back on leave in April 1946, nearing the end of The War, I played for Bristol City against Brentford in The Wartime Cup and had a great game. I was told after the match that a Newcastle scout had been watching me play and was very interested in me. That summer Bristol City went on tour to Denmark, but despite being in really good form, I found that I wasn't in the starting eleven for any of the tour games and had to make do with being a substitute. Subs were a new thing back then and were only used in friendlies, so I found the situation very confusing. In the first game I came on and scored two, but the next match, the same, no place in the side. That went on throughout the trip, but it all became clear on our return when I was told that Bristol City had agreed to transfer me to Newcastle for £8500 before we'd even left for Denmark. I travelled up and signed as quickly as I could.

I joined a fantastic forward line-up at St. James' Park, which is still considered by many as the best in the club's history. Jackie Milburn at outside-right, myself inside-right, Charlie Wayman, Len Shackleton and

Tommy Pearson. In Shackleton's first game that season we played New-port County at home and won 13-0, Len scored six. Being at St. James' Park really opened my eyes, I couldn't believe what passionate sup-porters they had. I wasn't even able to get on a bus without somebody insisting on paying my fare and if I walked past a shop or the market, the stall holders would run out to give me bags of fruit or meat. That was at a time when food was still being rationed. I found it embarrass-ing to be honest and ended up walking or running everywhere instead of having to face over-generous Geordies on the trolley-bus. Newcastle even had their own train which we used to travel to away matches on - it felt as if the players were treated like royalty! My only criticism of Newcastle fans was that they were so blinkered by their own team that they would never appreciate good play by the opponents, at Chelsea I found the supporters were far more appreciative of good football, whoever it was being played by. Newcastle fans have always given me a great reception when I've been back, even though I scored against them in almost every match after leaving St. James' Park.

I've never really spoken much about the real reason why I moved to Chelsea, but there was a lot of rubbish talked in the newspapers at the time which suggested that I had gone off the handle about a dirty bath in my digs and demanded a transfer. What a load of codswallop. The truth of the matter was that I was very unwell, I was putting so much energy into training and playing that I was virtually running on empty - I was diagnosed with the onset of consumption - tuburculosis as they call it nowadays. I'd lost so much weight that the Football League's own doctor was called in to look at me and he was concerned enough to recommend that Newcastle sent me away to recuperate. They decided to sell me for my own sake.

After a really thorough medical at Chelsea I was passed fit enough to sign, but I didn't do too well when I first arrived. I still remember one fan shouting at me that I was "no effing good, get back to New-castle". That comment made me so determined to get my strength back and to prove he was wrong, it spurred me on I suppose. Later on, after every goal or every win, I always looked over to where he stood and just stared. I can even picture the man's face today, over half a century later. The Chelsea manager, Billy Birrell, said very little about my form when I joined, he was obviously aware of my medical problems, but he was a gentleman and gave me the time I needed to get back to full fit-ness. He knew that wouldn't happen over night.

My luck changed near the end of the 1947-48 season, just before we were due to play Arsenal at Highbury. Believe it or not, Jimmy Bowie, our Scottish striker, somehow managed to fall off a snooker table and

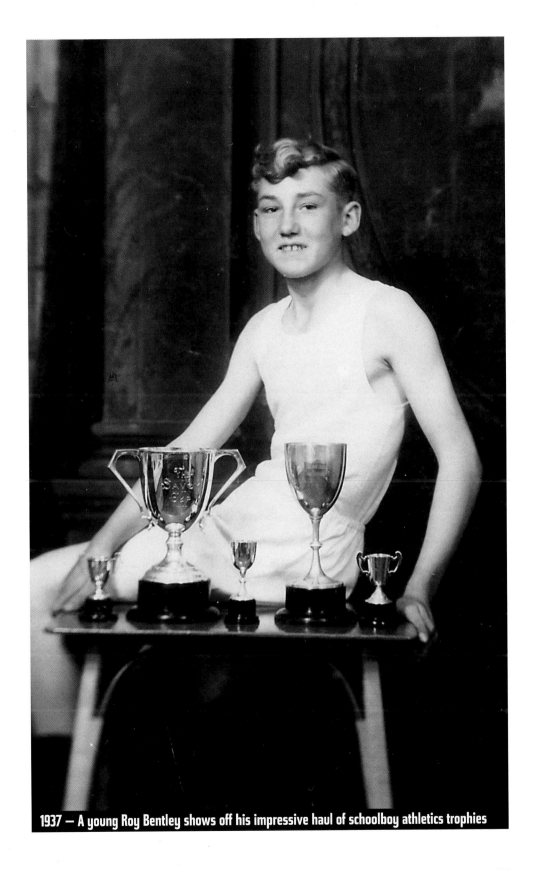

1937 – A young Roy Bentley shows off his impressive haul of schoolboy athletics trophies

1954 — Roy Bentley and Peter Sillett jog on the Stamford Bridge pitch during training

injured himself, so I was brought in. Jimmy came over to me before the game and said "there you go Roy, I've done you a right favour haven't I?" - little did I realise quite how big. That was the turning point for me, Chelsea played really well against Arsenal, I got a goal and we won two-nil. That gave me a big boost, so I trained hard all through the summer, doing lots of breathing exercises and running, then at last I started to put the muscle weight back on and feel like my old self again. After that I never looked back, I only missed two games during the whole of the 1949-50 season, scoring twenty-one goals and I remained the club's top scorer for the next seven years. The goals I started scoring for Chelsea also got me noticed by Walter Winterbottom the England manager and I made my debut against Sweden in May 1949, then played in the 1950 World Cup Finals in Brazil. As a kid I always dreamed of playing for England so it was an amazing moment when I received the telegram notifying me that I'd been called up.

Travelling to the World Cup Finals should have been an amazing experience, but because of our infamous defeat to the USA, it turned out to be somewhat of an embarrassing time. We were told after that humiliating 1-0 defeat not to talk about the match to the press and were ushered away straight after the game. We should have had three penalties that day and the game was played in an old bull ring officiated by the worst referee in the world. But people don't remember that, only the result. The press didn't want to hear those excuses in any case, we could have complained if we'd won ten-nil, but when you lose, explaining why is pointless sometimes.

The players' headquarters were set in a fantastic camp in the middle of the jungle, a wonderful complex which belonged to a mining company. We were surrounded by a beautiful rain forest, so the sights, sounds and smells were amazing. I also vividly remember the ice-cold mountain water that was piped straight into our showers, the water was so cold that the players could only manage a couple of seconds each after training. An American businessman recently informed me that I would fetch a great deal of money for the England cap I was given for playing in that USA game if I let it go to auction over in the States. I don't think they'll ever let us forget about that win in 1950!

But over all, I'm very proud of my England record, I scored nine goals in twelve internationals, which includes a hat-trick against Wales at Wembley in 1955. To have scored three goals in the shadow of the twin towers is quite a privilege. The reception I got from the Chelsea fans before the home game with Tottenham a few days later was just as fantastic, as I ran out on to the pitch there was a huge cheer and I thought, "what the hell is going on here?" As I looked around everyone was standing and cheering, I thought there was a presentation or award taking place on the pitch, but it still didn't dawn on me. Every time I touched the ball, another big cheer went up, then at the final whistle, the penny dropped that everyone inside Stamford Bridge was cheering me.

Ted Drake's arrival helped me significantly too as he brought in better training methods, more coaching and Chelsea became a more professionally organised club. In fact, Ted Drake was the greatest thing that could have happened to that club right then. I'm not just saying that because we won the Championship, but as soon as Ted arrived he changed the whole structure. But Ted almost didn't come to Stamford Bridge at all, he stalled on signing a contract for quite a while, even though he'd been offered the job. Ted wanted to be 100% sure he was able to achieve what he wanted at Chelsea, so he invited John Harris and myself out to play golf on five separate occasions to quiz us and to find out as much as he could about the club. I thought it was strange at first, that somebody would be unsure about joining a club like Chelsea from Reading, but after meeting him a few times, it became clear that he was just being thorough. Ted was making absolutely certain that he was able to implement everything he wanted at the club and that he stood the best possible chance of being a success at Stamford Bridge. When he eventually signed it was a big lift for everyone and in his first speech as manager he said he would need three years to form a team good enough to win something - which is exactly what he did.

We believed what our new manager had told us and Ted soon got the players to become more focussed, thinking about the game every second of the day and playing like a real team. Ted didn't want individuals in his side, he wanted us to play for each other, to become a family. Ted was also reluctant to sign any player who he wasn't completely certain about, even the fact that somebody wasn't married could be enough to put him off and Ted would drop his interest. Ted also had long talks with some of the existing players in which they were told to change their ways.

After Ted appointed me as Captain we used to spend hours together, before and after every game we'd have at least an hour talking about the previous match or what he wanted from the side during the game ahead. Ted expected me to be his link to the players and if a squad member had any problems at all, they would tell me and I would talk to Ted about them. My principle as Captain was never to speak about my team behind their backs, if I had a criticism about anyone's performance, I would always tell the player face to face before speaking to the manager about my gripes. That way I felt as though I was being fair to my teammates. There were also times that I had to tell players that they'd had a good game even when they'd had a bad one, I had to learn what made individuals tick and what approach motivated them to perform better. So my man management skills had to develop quickly and Ted Drake was a good mentor. The Manager would never tell a player how good he was, he would always talk about how much better they could become.

Ted had to retire early from playing football because of terrible back troubles, a condition that continued, meaning he had to endure extensive physiotherapy every day at Stamford Bridge to allow him to move around properly, but he would never let on to the other players what kind of pain he was in. Ted's hard work, not to mention the improved attitude of the players, started to pay off during the 1953-54 season and we felt as if we were becoming a top side. The belief that we could win something had started to emerge.

I felt at home at Chelsea, it was a great club to be at, my family had settled in well and we moved into a nice house near Hanger Lane. The other players were a great bunch, especially Chelsea stalwart John Harris. John had been at the club for years and we both got on really well. John used to carry a bible around with him everywhere, he was a very religious man, and when I eventually replaced him as club Captain, I think we became even closer. He was as good a friend as anyone could have been, and at one stage, I thought he was going to become part of my family.

Despite his religious beliefs, John was a hard, hard man on the pitch. His biggest rival in the game was Manchester United's Jack Rowley and they really used to go at each other during a game. I remember one match, when Manchester United were still sharing at Manchester City's Maine Road ground after The War, the two of them went to ground after a heavy challenge. While they were on the floor Rowley rubbed mud and lime from the pitch markings into John's face. Well, the lime got in his eyes and he couldn't see properly, but he just got up and wagged his finger as if to say 'you don't do that kind of thing to me'! When United next got a corner I came back to help defend. As we all jumped for the ball I went in hard and so did John. Very hard. To give him his due, Rowley tried to get up, but he was gasping for air and couldn't talk. From then on, every game the two came up against each other, they really used to whack it out.

I had a few run-ins with Bolton's Malcolm Barrass too, but I knew he wasn't up for it. Normally he was the kind of player who would kick you up in the air and kick you again on the way back down, but I remember his team mate, Nat Lofthouse, telling me on an England trip that I had him worried. When we played them at Burnden Park during the Championship season we beat them five-two and he didn't get near me all

1953 — Chelsea Captain Roy Bentley let's fly with his trusty right boot

match after I told him before we kicked off that I had his card marked. Chelsea ran Bolton ragged that day - I got two, Seamus O'Connell got one, Peter Sillett scored from the spot and one of the Bolton lads put into his own net.

Ted's first signing, John McNichol, was great for me, although John was as much a part of the machine as everyone else, his passes suited me and we built a good partnership. But Johnny was more of a supply line than a centre-forward partner as he had been when we played together in Newcastle's second team. Hugh Billington played well up front in the space I created in the early 1950s, but he didn't really have the physique or pace to be consistently outstanding, so Les Stubbs was brought in by Ted. Les was a good foil for me and knew when to make intelligent runs and which post to attack at corners. Because we were getting such great service from Eric Parsons and Frank Blunstone on the wings Les and I had plenty of opportunities to score.

We played in the old WM formation, and because Ted was always screaming at us to attack, the boss expected his wingers to drop back really deep to pick the ball up - what we'd call wing-backs today. After a while Ted asked the pair to drop back even deeper, to collect the ball inside our own half. Eric Parsons was a real character and was always joking, so he asked if Ted wanted them to start taking goal kicks too!

Eric Parsons also chipped in with some great goals that season, he was great at volleying the ball from the edge of the area and scored some real crackers. Eric must have been one of the unluckiest men in football during the mid-50s, he was one of the best around, but because Stanley Matthews and Tom Finney were still playing and were established internationals, Eric didn't get a real chance to prove himself on the International stage. 'Rabbit' did play for the 'B' team, I remember him travelling to Holland with Peter Sillett and myself who had been selected for the full side. He played a blinder I thought, but that became Eric's only opportunity to represent his country, which I think is a great shame.

I scored twenty-one goals in the season we won the title and the wingers played a big part in helping me reach that total. I also seemed to score a lot of my goals when the pitches were at their worst, between November and February. I'm not quite sure why the heavy, water saturated ball and muddy or frozen pitches suited me better, but I scored eight goals in seven games between New Year's Day and the beginning of March 1955.

I thought Seamus O'Connell was another impressive finisher too, but he wasn't really around long enough to judge properly. His record during the Championship season was eight in eleven games, but because he was an amateur and was only at Chelsea for the one season, he never proved what kind of footballer he could have become. I would have liked it if he could have trained with Chelsea every day because it was clear the lad had potential. Seamus scored a hat-trick on his debut against Manchester United in a game we lost six-five. I remember that match as clear as anything, if only we had another twenty minutes extra time we would have won it! Chelsea never gave up that day and right up until the end we thought we could get something out of the match, that was the kind of spirit we had.

As the season reached the half way stage, the players were looking forward to every game and we started to believe we were the best side around. We'd only ever think that inwardly, we were never flash or boastful, but there was certainly an inner belief that emerged and I knew the lads were up for it - Ted Drake believed in us all along too. In a season where Chelsea's first team won the Championship the reserves and the youth teams also won their respective leagues, so apart from the F.A. Cup, Chelsea won everything there was to win in 1955 - including the Charity Shield.

Some people in the game think that it's more difficult for a centre-forward to captain the side than it is for a central defender or a midfielder, but because I liked to drop back and help defend, I could still bark out my orders and keep the players on their toes. I nearly always came back to help defend corners, so I didn't have to rely on other players to help me communicate with the defenders. Ted would often say that if I led by example, then it made captaining the side that much easier because the other players see how you're playing and match your effort.

One of the best Captains I ever played against, and somebody I used to study very closely, was Manchester United's John Carey. It was like United had an extra player in their side when Johnny played and he captained Manchester and Ireland for many years. As a Captain it's very difficult to think about what your team-mates should be doing and motivating them whilst still concentrating on your own game, but Johnny Carey could do that better than any other player from that era. I would watch him organising his players, positioning them as he wanted, pushing people wider or deeper, but still have a blinder himself. John was a truly great footballer.

There weren't any bust-ups on the field between the Chelsea lads either and I can't recall any dissent from the players towards me. I hardly ever swore on the pitch, that was a lesson I learned early from my Dad, he always told me that the kind of players who shouted their mouths off and swore every other word were poor communicators and they couldn't express themselves in any other way. From a Captain's per-

'Up The Champs' — A mascot waits as the team run out to clinch the title led by Bentley

April 1955 — Roy Bentley heads home in the final game of the season at Old Trafford

December 1954 — Bentley scores at Molineux in The Blues' memorable 4-3 win

spective my life was made that much easier because I had great players around me in 1954 and 1955.

The two goalkeepers that were used, Chick Thomson and Bill Robertson, were as identical as you could ever have hoped for in their consistency. Chick was probably the more agile of the two because of his slighter build, although Bill was more confident when coming out to collect crosses and a little stronger in the air because he had that extra bit of weight behind him. When big centre-forwards came clattering in, Bill was better equipped and they bounced off him, but Ted found it almost impossible to pick one ahead of the other. The Manager insisted that the 'keepers controlled the defenders in front of him, but the quality we had in those positions made life easier for them.

Peter Sillett at right-back had possibly his most impressive season for Chelsea in 1954, he put in a huge amount of effort to prove that Ted Drake had made the right decision when he brought him up from Southampton. He wasn't the best of trainers, perhaps, but at 6ft 2in and fourteen stone, few opponents got round him. Peter's pace was surprising for a tall lad, his take-off was deceptive, he didn't look that quick, but once he was moving he was fast and other players had trouble reading him. Peter had great positional sense too, he was very strong in the tackle and once he'd won the ball his distribution was excellent. It's no exaggeration to say that he could pass accurately over a distance of more than a hundred yards - he had a huge kick on him and I was often the target.

Left-back, Stan Willemse, on the other side was ideal too. Stan had the reputation of being a hard man, but there was more to his game than his robustness. He wasn't a dirty player, Stan just loved a battle on the pitch and was a great worker - he proved his versatility in other positions during the course of the Championship too. He had a great left foot and I think Stan would be a great player today as a wing-back, he was quick, could take knocks, plus he got stuck in. But I think it's always difficult to compare players from different eras, and Chelsea have had some real greats over the years. I wasn't too offended when Zola was recently voted the best Chelsea player of all time. He was absolute class, and to do what he did at his age was a remarkable achievement. But I always separate great players into different periods, I think you can only compare players five years or so apart.

Ken Armstrong was the kind of player any football manager would love and along with his counterpart, Derek Saunders, they gave everything they had in every game. Even on an off day they would never stop trying, in the WM formation, there were no better wing-half in the country that year.

Three players shared the centre-half position en route to the title, John Harris, Ron Greenwood plus Stan Wicks and all of them were very reliable defenders. John was a bit past his best, but still played more than thirty games that season. Ron Greenwood was a really stylish centre-half, but too fair a player at times I thought. If you had his ability football-wise, mixed with Stan Willemse's bite, you'd have the best defender in the country without a shadow of a doubt. Ron was also a very likeable guy and we used to travel in to training together on the tube most days. I used to catch the train at Park Royal, meet Ron at Greenford, then talk football all the way in to Stamford Bridge and all the way home again. Ron was football potty, he studied formations and tactics and of course he eventually went on to manage West Ham United, then the England team. Ron took it quite badly when Ted decided to bring Stan Wicks into the side and he left for Fulham almost straight away - Ron took it as a big personal blow. But Ted knew that there was something slightly lacking in that department and he proved that if you want to get to the top in football, you have to be prepared to make tough decisions.

Stan Wicks' relationship with Ted from their time at Reading, added to the fact that he was a fitness fanatic and equipped to slot straight into the side, proved to be a master stroke. Stan Wicks and myself got on so well from day one, we were on the same wavelength, but he didn't have the best of home debuts if I remember. Stan made a bit of a hash during the two-one win against Tottenham, I saw his head drop. I knew the mistake had affected him quite badly, so I gave him a gee-up. "Come on Stan", I said, "don't worry, we all make mistakes, you'll make a few more than that before the season's over, now chin up!"

A debut at a new club is so important for a player, I couldn't allow Stan to blow the incident out of proportion. I scored the equaliser not long afterwards and Stan was so delighted he kept thanking me and tried to kiss me, which I was having none of! I said "what's the matter with you Stan!" to which he replied, "I'm just so happy that I haven't cost us the game and Ted won't have as big a go at me afterwards." From that moment on, though, Stan did everything right at Chelsea, he was first selected to play for the Football League representative side, then for England. In fact I think he deserved more recognition than he got from his time in football, but in the end he had to retire because of injury. The pair of us became very close, we teamed up again when I managed Reading later on and we used to go away on holidays together. Stan was an amazing man and was so brave during his battle with cancer, I was the only person who knew for a long time that he was battling the disease.

April 1955 — The new Champions are clapped out by Manchester United at Old Trafford

April 1955 — Ted Drake shakes hands with his Captain after claiming the title crown

Apart from the individual who gave me a hard time when I first joined, I've always found Chelsea fans a great bunch. Running out on to the old Stamford Bridge pitch and seeing the applause spread round the whole bowl, all the way up to The Shed at the back, really did make you glow. Even when we were battling against relegation it always felt that the crowd was behind us. But when we were doing well and the ground was packed with more than 70,000 fans, it was something else.

My first experience of a packed Stamford Bridge was in October 1948 against Blackpool on a Wednesday afternoon in the pouring rain. Most people only worked a half day on Wednesdays in those days, but I would imagine a fair few had also skipped off work too. There were so many people inside the ground [77,000] that people had spilled out of the stands and were sitting on the dog track. Chelsea got a late equaliser and the match finished three-all - Stanley Matthews and Stan Mortensen were playing against us. The noise is different inside the ground now, the stands are so high it feels like the atmosphere created from the fans is coming from above your head. The crowd was very cosmopolitan in the late Forties and early Fifties, almost every famous show-biz name passing through London seemed to be drawn to Stamford Bridge - but Ted didn't like the reputation the club had earned as a theatre stars Saturday afternoon hang-out. Dickie Attenborough came to train with the players once, but he has always remained loyal to the club, Dickie is as fanatical about Chelsea now as he was all that time ago.

The Championship was won thanks to our amazing run from Christmas until the end of the season. I think the state of the Stamford Bridge pitch could have played a part during the winter months too, but luck is just as important - all Champions need a decent slice of that at some stage during the season. So when the consistency of the emerging players improved too, Chelsea got stronger and stronger. Ted and I often talked about the number of players that a good team could 'carry', early on there were possibly one or two players who weren't quite up to scratch and the rest of the side had to compensate for them, but after Christmas everyone was on song. Defeats became draws and draws became wins. There were fewer points dropped and Chelsea ran up an unbeaten run of ten games in the closing weeks. Manchester United and Wolves simply couldn't compete with us after Christmas and New Year.

The F.A. Cup games of 1954-55 have become a bit of a blur over the years, that is why I admire the likes of Arsenal and Manchester United now because they seem to be capable of winning the Championship, while being consistent enough to seriously challenge in other competitions too. To win a title and a cup is a tremendous achievement, whoever the team.

The scenes when we clinched the title, following the home win against Sheffield Wednesday, will always stay with me. Looking out from the balcony over thousands of fans was a special moment, but there were no presentations, just introductions and speeches.

As Captain I said a few words, thanking all the players for their efforts and expressing my appreciation for players like John Harris and Ron Greenwood. They had both played a significant part in what we'd achieved, but weren't involved in clinching the title at the end of the season. Looking at the joy on the faces of the Chelsea fans made the season complete. I felt so grateful that I was able to achieve my ambition of winning a Championship medal at Stamford Bridge and I think I am prouder of that achievement than winning my England caps.

Ron
Greenwood

December 1954 — Ron Greenwood in aerial combat against Wolves during Chelsea's 4-3 win

Ron Greenwood and Derek Saunders enjoy themselves at the races on tour in America

Ron was a classy footballer with a commanding, 'all is well' feeling about him on the pitch and I would have liked to have seen him at Chelsea a good deal longer, as I feel the club could have used his potential in a far greater way. Greenwood would never 'hoof' the ball unless he absolutely had to. Perhaps some of the less experienced players didn't feel comfortable alongside a player with so much confidence, but he was such a good ball player. Ron was also a footballing intellectual and studied the game very closely which paid dividends after he retired from playing when he went on to manage West Ham United, and then, of course, England. Ron is currently living down on the south coast but was unfortunately not well enough to be interviewed for this book.

Albert Sewell

Charlie
Thomson

I t was almost inevitable that I was going to become a goalkeeper, my father had been a professional 'keeper for twenty-two years, playing with Brighton mostly, and I'd been crawling around dressing rooms since the age of three. There were also two Scottish internationals on my mother's side of the family, so football was always part of my life. Later on Dad was able to offer his critical opinion on my performances, and drawing on his vast experience, he helped me improve my game.

The strange thing was, considering football was in my blood, I was sent to an academy school in Perth where 'soccer' was really frowned upon. We had a sports master who was a real snob and only allowed Rugby to be played. In some ways I think it may have done me good to play Rugby more than football at that age, especially as a budding goalie, because one way or another I learned to take a lot of knocks without getting too excited about them. Also, handling funny shaped balls made catching round ones easier later in life I reckon.

At school we had to play all our football unofficially on Saturday mornings, and because of the lack of practice, we were useless. Our team lost by more than ten goals most games and I was playing at right-half. In one match things got so bad that we were losing nine-nil at half time, so it was decided that because I was the tallest, I should go in goal for the second half. We only conceded two more during the next forty-five minutes, my team were quite chuffed with me in goal, so it was decided that should be where I played from then on.

Football became more serious from around the age of fifteen, I'd been playing for the local YMCA, which contained players ranging all the way up to forty, and in 1946 a lot of ex-professionals were playing in our league. That didn't do me any harm at all. After that I joined another amateur team called Blairgowrie, who were well known for 'dropping something' in your boot if you had a good game - and it was soon after joining that I got my lucky break.

We were playing a team called Newton Grange Star in the Scottish Junior Cup, just outside Edinburgh, when I was spotted by a scout from Clyde who had got on the wrong bus and ended up at our match by mistake. I'm glad it wasn't a completely wasted trip for him, as I signed a professional contract with the Division A side a week after his visit. Life at Clyde was very good, I had started work as a trainee engineer and the club allowed me to continue my apprenticeship and I played football at the weekends. My boss at the engineering works was very understanding and he let me off work to go to training most mornings.

One Thursday evening the Clyde youngsters were playing a training match against the club's journeymen, but the game was interrupted when we saw a police car drive up and park next to the pitch. Every-one stopped as the two officers got out and walked over to us. I was shocked when they asked, "which one of you is Charles Thomson?" My first thought was that one of my family had been involved in an accident, so you can imagine my relief when it transpired that Clyde had asked the police to help track me down because we had no telephone at our house. The club needed to let me know that I had been called up to the first team to face Rangers in the Charity Cup Final at Hampden Park the next day. My heart started racing there and then.

Looking back at the day now, I have no idea how I coped at that age, I was just a naïve boy really. The Rangers team we faced was idolised, and on reflection, it is easier to name their line-up than my own team's. I'll always remember the game, Clyde did really well, leading two-nil at one stage, but then Rangers were awarded two penalty kicks and forced a replay - which we lost three-two. Things were going well for me at Shawfield, but the inevitable happened and I had to serve my National Service, which saw me based a long way from home, just outside Aldershot in Hampshire.

It was unbelievable, there were thirty-three professional footballers in our Army unit and when I arrived in Hampshire, I discovered that our Major had more than just a soft spot for football. He called me in to see him soon after arriving and told me that he'd allow me to travel back to Scotland every weekend to play for Clyde, which was a fantastic gesture. I left barracks on Thursday nights to catch the over-night sleeper North, returning on the Monday morning following a match. I won the Army Cup during my time in the forces and I learned later it was during that run that Ted Drake spotted me while he was managing Reading.

After I was demobbed in July 1952 I only played three more games for Clyde before becoming a Chelsea player - the move followed a rather unfortunate bust-up with the Chairman. We had just lost five-three in terrible conditions and were sitting in the dressing room after the game. I shouldn't have played that day as I was suffering from bronchitis and had dragged myself out of bed to turn out - but none of the goals were my fault. Our manager, Paddy Travers, normally locked the dressing room door after games, so it was just him and the players, but that day he didn't and the Chairman burst in and started shouting and abusing the team one by one. I was just pulling my mud-caked, yellow jersey off when he started laying into me, which turned out to be a mistake because I just flipped and threw the filthy shirt in his face, then tried to throttle him with it. The other players thought it was hilarious, but the manager told me that I'd shot my bolt at the club and was on the way out after humiliating the Chairman. A short time afterwards Ted Drake sent his assistant, Stewart Davidson, up to talk to me and I signed a contract the following day. Rochdale and Portsmouth were also keen on me signing at the time, but following a chat with my father, there was only one worth considering - it didn't take us long to weigh up the pros and cons of each club. In any case I didn't see my future in Scotland at all to be honest. There were no agents or representatives to deal with contracts in those days, a player had to fend for himself, so having an ex-professional father to offer his advice was a big help to me. My only real demand was that Chelsea paid me top money throughout the year, which meant that my wages remained the same even during the close season.

I arrived in London on a Thursday and was taken straight to my digs in Britannia Road, where I became one of Bobby Smith's many Chelsea bed partners! I didn't stay there too long and moved out to Motspur Park in Surrey, living in a house owned by the guy who used to run the Tote board behind the goal at Stamford Bridge. I shared with two reserves, Alan Rowland and a South African, Laurie Mitchell. Although the travelling was a bit of a bind, life was good and I settled in well, living in bustle of the capital put five yards on my speed because I had to cross the road a lot quicker than I did up in Scotland!

The social scene was good, there was a group of four or five of us who used to go out to the cinema or theatre and we used to go to watch the ice hockey at Earls Court a lot too. None of the players I knocked around with were big drinkers, we used to have the odd beer, but nobody used to go out and get plastered. Being young players, trying to make the grade, we were as keen as mustard and were more into our training than our boozing. We would never have survived training with a hangover in any case, pounding up and down the steps on those huge Stamford Bridge terraces and being pushed through the pain barrier was bad enough under normal circumstances, let alone a splitting headache. Training at Chelsea was always very, very hard.

But it was always amusing when we returned to the club for pre-season training after the summer, all the players would be divided into three squads depending on how much weight they had put on during the close season. All the guys who wouldn't put a pound on, no matter how much they ate, were in group one, I was in the middle group and those who'd heaped on the weight, players like Bill, would go straight into the heavy squad. The hefty boys would really be put through their paces and I recall Bobby Smith being made to run around in a plastic suit with jumpers on top and secured with elastic to make him sweat more.

Chelsea treated us fantastically, even to the point where we were wrapped in cotton wool to a certain extent. But there was a lot of

1954 — Edwards, Dicks & Thomson take a breather during training

February 1955 — Chick, Harris & Greenwood watch as Huddersfield score at The Bridge

1955 — Chick studies a ball while McNichol practices his juggling skills at Hayes Town

discipline and the players were well aware who was the boss - Ted Drake was a man's man and if he said anything you were under no illusion that he meant it. I'll never forget finding out the hard way in training one Monday morning. Following a defensive blunder up at Middlesbrough the previous weekend, between Ken Armstrong and 'keeper Bill Robertson, Ted had put up a big sign in the dressing room which proclaimed; "Goal-keepers Will Not Throw The Ball, Repeat, Will Not Throw The Ball!"

But throwing the ball out to a defender becomes almost second nature to goalies and in training the following Tuesday, in a practice match, I simply forgot about the new sign. I caught a ball from Bobby Campbell and threw it straight to Eric Parsons, he tore down the wing, crossed it to Roy Bentley, who nodded it into the net. By the time the ball had hit the back of the net Ted Drake was marching towards me bellowing, "can't you bloody read!?!" I said "but we scored from my throw..." He replied, "I don't give a damn...", I didn't play the following match! Ted had no favourites, apart from Roy Bentley perhaps, and if you stepped over the mark you'd get pulled up, no matter who you were.

Even when I wasn't falling out with the manager, Tuesday mornings were always eventful because we all used to sit down and watch the previous match played back to us on film in the games room and have all our mistakes pointed out to us by the coaching staff. It was so funny, watching your team mates cringe as the attention switched from one to the next, listening to the commentary saying things like, "Johnny McNichol, why are you walking back to the half way line?" Then I'd see a shot whistle past my post with me rooted to the spot and I'd slide down my seat in embarrassment as the commentator, Albert Tennant, exclaimed "where were you there Charlie?"

Every player had to explain their actions on the pitch and the exercise was to underline the levels expected from the manager and to make us aware that even minor imperfections in our game would be picked up and noted. What I liked about Chelsea was the fact that things were done in a positive way, there was no bawling and screaming, Ted and his coaches liked to gee you up rather than dress you down and most of the lads respected that. Roy Bentley was just like that too, on the pitch he was always encouraging the players and I thought he was an excellent Captain.

Because Ted was such a prolific striker during his playing career, he would often have a bit of fun with the goalkeepers. Sometimes he'd come up and put his arm around me in training and say, "did I ever tell you about the day when I put seven goals past Aston Villa's goalie?" I respected Ted for what he was, a rough diamond in many respects, but his heart was as big as he was and very generous with it.

One day I was up in his office, sorting out my cup tickets while I was out with a broken finger, when he spotted a young kid walking into the ground. Ted had a huge window behind his desk that overlooked the whole back of the stadium and I remember him saying to me, "who is that?" It was a fifteen-year-old youngster who had come down from the north for a trial at Chelsea, but he looked a right state. "That can't do him any good", said Ted, "just imagine how he feels having to turn up at a club like Chelsea looking like a down and out." He called his secretary, Mrs. Metcalf, and raised some petty cash and I was asked to take the kid up to Simpson's in Piccadilly to get him some new clothes - underwear, socks, shoes, trousers, coat, jacket, the lot. The kid thought he had won the pools!

My Chelsea debut came in a one-all draw up at Stoke, played on the heaviest pitch I think I've ever seen. I'll always remember Bobby Smith trying to run with the ball on the boggy ground, then he'd try and thump the ball forwards, only for it to stop a couple of yards further ahead of him. The conditions were so poor that I had to ask my defenders to stand near the edge of the penalty area because the ball was like a lump of lead and there was a breeze blowing straight back at me. They all spread themselves around the eighteen yards box and I tried to find one of them. I don't know if you've ever tried to kick one of those old leather balls, but it took some doing!

There were a lot of clubs who used to 'treat' the balls that the opposition players practiced with before the game too, and there were a lot of injuries picked up just before the kick-off. Clyde used to blow the balls up brick hard, then put them in a bath with a plank on top so they would be full of water. If you had a slight ankle or knee injury going into the game, the warm up would make it a damn sight worse. Trying to catch a ball like that stung like crazy too. Being a goalkeeper in those conditions, and in an era when there was little or no protection from either the rules or the referee, was a treacherous business. Players were allowed to shoulder-barge the 'keeper, but there were always elbows, knees and boots to deal with too. There were a fair few times that I would somersault through the air after being caught late following a high catch, and on one occasion, I did a double back flip and almost ended up in the crowd after being walloped by Everton's Dave Hickson.

It was rough in those eighteen-yard boxes, especially as I was built like a pencil. I spent a lot of time in training learning how to protect myself because it can be quite daunting when you see a centre-forward running straight at you with only one thing in mind. Some referees would come into the dressing room before the game and remind all the players that football was a man's game, which was like a red rag to a bull as far as some players were concerned, but others would tell the goalies that they would be protected. In practice, though, their compassion normally only meant that when we got hurt they'd let the stretcher come on slightly quicker!

In those situations communication is very important and I always had an arrangement with my full-backs and centre-halves where they would tell me to catch or punch the ball depending on how much time they thought I had and who was about to clatter into me. But no matter how much warning colleagues gave me, injuries were inevitable. I had four of my front teeth smashed out up at Bolton by Nat Lofthouse's left elbow, they had snapped across the middle and I remember looking about in the mud for the bits. It was a freezing day too and every time I drew breath the pain was amazing. As soon as I got back to London, Chelsea sent me straight to a dental surgeon who extracted the stumps and inserted four false ones. Can you imagine my face when my landlady cooked me a steak for my dinner that night!

Dead legs were the most common injury during a match because forwards were allowed to chase 'keepers around the box and knock into them, nowadays if an opponent even looks at a goalie the referee blows his whistle. I also picked up one or two cracked ribs, a broken nose and a fair few broken fingers during my time in the game - if you could see some of my bent finger tips today you would realise how hard the balls really were. Sustaining a broken finger would normally only keep you out for three games, which when you consider there were no protective 'wicket keeper's' gloves, seems remarkable today. I used to have my string gloves made for me, but they weren't padded and I had to have an elastic band wrapped round them to keep them on. My goalkeeper's kit was atrocious too, old boots, scruffy shorts, a woollen jumper and an old flat cap, which was the source of great amusement for a lot of people. It was a terrible looking hat, but I wore it for many, many years and eventually auctioned it off for charity. I think it raised about £20! Another injury I remember was when an Aston Villa full-back hit a shot from just outside the area that dipped just as I was about to catch it and hit me just above the knees. I thought the ball had broken both my legs as I was in so much pain. I had two vivid bruises on my thighs for about ten days afterwards - I can't imagine a modern 'beach ball' leaving the same impressions.

There was a lot of competition for the goalkeeper's position at Stamford Bridge when I arrived, there were seven goalies on the books, ranging from Bill Robertson and Harry Medhurst, myself, then four youngsters coming through the ranks - Chelsea were competing in so many leagues back then. I eventually took over from Harry as Bill's deputy and we seemed to share the first team spot depending on which one of us got injured. It was like that for almost four seasons. We both seemed to be very consistent in our form over that period and I would say that there was only one time when we were both dropped because of a dip in performances. In the Championship season we seemed to share the goalie's jersey, admittedly Bill played a lot more games than me, but I was in goal throughout the exciting run-in to winning the title from Christmas onwards.

I had a very good relationship with Bill, being a fellow Scot helped I think, but neither of us were edgy about who should be the first choice 'keeper and we used to look out for each other. Bill never seemed to have a lot to say, but when he did he was a genuine and honest individual - he was a big, friendly soul. I had a great deal of respect for him as a person and as a friend - I liked him an awful lot. Bill had the same attitude to training as big Peter Sillett, he didn't like it very much, especially the running, but we spent a lot of time together in the gym and practicing goalkeeper's drills. Bill and I saw each other as teammates not rivals.

An example of this came later on when Ted Drake bought the England goalie, Reg Matthews, from Coventry - a player who couldn't hold a candle to Bill in my opinion. This meant that Bill and myself were either going to be twelfth man at best, or in the reserves. Instead of the situation dividing us, though, it brought us even closer and we both went to see Ted together to ask for a transfer at exactly the same time. I vividly remember walking up and tentatively knocking on the Manager's office door at the ground, then seeing the wry smile on Ted's face as we approached his desk. He knew full well that we weren't happy with the situation and after saying our piece, we asked if there was any chance of a transfer. He just looked at us both and said, "who the hell is going to want to buy you two?" We all had a good laugh and joke about it and came to an agreement that if anybody came in, Bill would get first choice. Bill had a couple of clubs express an interest but he decided to stay at The Bridge, then Nottingham Forest came in for me which is where I won an F.A. Cup Winner's medal to go with my Chelsea Championship honour.

Even before Matthews arrived it became increasingly frustrating for me not to be in the first team every week, everyone wants to be involved in the big match. Not being picked wouldn't make me pull my hair out with rage or anything, but at that stage of my career playing second fiddle to anyone wasn't a satisfactory situation. Chelsea had a fantastic reserve team, who played in front of crowds of about eight thousand, so it could have been worse, but first team football had to be my priority.

1953 – Charlie Thomson claws the air as a Birmingham City shot whistles over

1954 – Charlie's team-mate, Bill Robertson, dives full length at The Bridge

April 1955 — Stubbs & Bentley watch as Pompy's keeper saves in the draw at Fratton Park

1959 — Chick catches during the Nottingham Forest - Luton Town Cup Final at Wembley

There were some great defenders in front of me when I was in the first team; Peter Sillett, with the least amount of effort, was a great full-back and with Ken Armstrong in front of him, they formed an impressive combination. I'll always remember Peter sinking that penalty in the game against Wolves at Stamford Bridge near the end of the Championship season - to step up and take a spot kick in that situation really took some bottle. Peter had a superb game that day, he was up against Johnny Hancock, who was a cracking little player, but Sillett made sure he didn't get a kick for almost the entire match. The only time Hancock got past him was in the last ten minutes when he managed to get a good shot in. Fortunately I got a good look at it coming and got down to tip the ball onto the foot of the post, which jangled the nerves of over seventy-five thousand fans. Everything was riding on that game, Chelsea had to beat Wolves if we were serious Championship material, but strangely I don't recall any of the players being too nervous before the match. Ted Drake was rumoured to have been up all the previous night, walking around Wimbledon Common unable to sleep. Apparently he came back in the morning slightly bedraggled, but the players seemed calm. Those make or break games are great because they are the ones that make being a footballer so special.

As the season came to a close and Chelsea were tightening their grip on the title, I shared a railway carriage with Ted Drake and his trainer, Jack Oxbury, on the way down to Portsmouth. With just three games to go until the end of the season they were talking about what was needed from each game to win the title. They had really started to believe that the crown was going to be ours and it was fascinating listening to them going through all the permutations and what they thought our rivals would get out of their remaining fixtures. It had never entered my head before that moment, but it suddenly dawned on me that I may not have played enough games to qualify for a Championship medal if we won the League, so I interrupted what they were saying and asked them if they knew. "How many games have you got to play to get a medal?" I piped up. "You're playing it today" was Ted's reply, which was a massive relief for me. I made a couple of important saves that afternoon and we should have wrapped up the title there and then. Les Stubbs [pictured top left] had a perfectly good goal disallowed near the end, which meant we had to settle for a draw.

Looking back at some of the saves I made for Chelsea reminds me of a penalty I faced against Arsenal in 1955. As their left-back walked up I remembered facing him before, during an Army Cup Quarter Final a few years earlier. I always kept notes on which way certain players took penalties and my memory came up trumps, I saved his shot again.

1955 — Charlie makes his finger-tips penalty save at Highbury against Arsenal

That was special to me, we loved beating Arsenal. In fact there was a big photo spread of that save used in the following month's Picture Post [pictured left]. Back then penalties weren't given as freely as they are now and goalkeepers didn't face quite as many as our contemporaries do, so my little notebook came in useful on more than one occasion. But if a player thumped the ball well, a 'keeper didn't really stand much chance of stopping a ball of that weight.

I was fortunate enough to have played at a time when some of football's true greats were still plying their trade, and depending which way you look at it, I had the pleasure and misfortune of finding out just how great some of them really were. For example I'll never forget being beaten by Len Shackleton when he was with Sunderland, he scored a goal past me that still baffles me today. In the first half I came rushing out to narrow the angle after he'd been played through on goal, he shaped to shoot to my left and looked the same way, but he shot to my right and I had to save with my toes. Later in the game we found ourselves in exactly the same situation, so I rushed out again, stood up as long as I could, watched his body shape, but he sold me again and the ball flew into the net. He was a truly brilliant footballer, as was Stanley Matthews, but Shackleton doesn't get the same exposure.

Chelsea's Ian MacFarlane clobbered Blackpool's Stanley Matthews about twenty minutes before half time one year and Stan had to go off. The Stamford Bridge crowd didn't like it one bit and they booed Ian at the break. Some of the other Chelsea players pulled him up for the challenge back in the dressing room too and said he was out of order. Anyway, we came out for the second half and Matthews was still missing from the Blackpool side, then, about ten minutes later, a huge cheer came up and Matthews came back on. At the end of the match MacFarlane was crying, partly through frustration, partly through temper and guilt, because Stan toyed with Ian and made him look like an absolute idiot with some of his tricks. Matthews didn't say a word when he was hurt or carried off, but as soon as he returned, he held his hand up in the air and demanded the ball so he could run at Ian again and again.

Talking of tough tackles, a rock in that Championship winning side was Stan Willemse, a fearsome player and great left-back. I think the Chelsea team were as frightened of Stan as the opposition were, and he was an unmistakable sight with his sleeves rolled up and his shorts pulled high. On his own admission, Stan wouldn't last ten minutes in today's game, he would have been sent off week in week out, but he was a useful footballer too.

Big Stan Wicks at centre-half was another player who I enjoyed having in front of me, his introduction took so much pressure off the goalkeepers. Jack Saunders and Ron Greenwood, who had played there before Stan were both good defenders, but I felt more confident with Wicksy there. Stan was like a big tree trunk in that defence, he would win so much in the air, which meant I didn't have to come out and catch everything. Ron Greenwood was a thinking man's footballer, he loved his theories, but he left Chelsea under a slight cloud, which showed there wasn't a lot of sentiment. When it was time for you to go, it was time for you to go.

Players were only offered yearly contracts back then and when the retained list was due to be announced, near the end of the season, groups of trainees, along with some of the younger players, would hang around the office at Stamford Bridge. The second and third team players would wait for the first team squad to finish training so they could ask us if we knew anything more than they did. "Have you had a letter yet?" they would ask. It was quite a desperate situation for them because there wasn't much time to sort out a new job if they discovered they weren't being kept on the books.

Another thing I found memorable about our Chelsea side was that it wasn't a team full of individuals, we were a close-knit unit who worked hard together to achieve what we did. There was no fuss, no tantrums, no players who thought they were better than the rest - everybody did what was expected of them to the best of their abilities and reaped the reward through hard graft.

The crowd was always good to me at Chelsea, I got the impression that they trusted me between the sticks, but away from Stamford Bridge fans were less friendly. I always found Everton the most hostile ground to visit, apart from one old lady that is, who used to hand me a bag of toffees before the match. She was a dear old soul who always stood just behind my left post, but it seemed as if everyone else behind the goal enjoyed giving the opponent's goalie a tough old time. I remember one day, during a F.A. Cup Fifth Round tie at Goodison in 1956, a man who was standing close to the old dear had pushed his flask between the railings, onto the track around the pitch for safe keeping. But he must have regretted doing so after Johnny McNichol smashed it to smith-ereens with a shot that went just wide. When we swapped ends after the interval I heard the guy shout out to the old lady "if you give him any more sweets I'll give you what for..." We lost one-nil. Cardiff was another place I didn't like visiting very much, some of the kids used to fill paper bags up with gravel and throw them at my net, which was really annoying.

After the final game of the season, at Old Trafford against Manchester United, a few of the lads tried to wind Ted Drake up about having placed bets against Chelsea, but The Guv'nor didn't fall for it. We went straight over to Ireland after the season finished to play against Shamrock Rovers, which proved to be a fantastic trip because in 1955 food was still rationed in England. Over in Ireland we could eat as much butter, cream and meat as we liked and I think the players stuffed themselves while we were there. Maybe that's why we lost the match.

Not only were the Championship celebrations almost completely flat, but we had to wait until near the start of the following season for our medals, even though the players didn't expect much fuss, some would have been nice I think. Looking back, it was a pity that the fans didn't see any trophies presented at Stamford Bridge, because after witnessing the Forest fan's faces when I was in their team that won the 1959 Cup Final at Wembley, it made me realise what the Stamford Bridge diehards had missed out on. Our medals were eventually distributed in the board room over lunch by Chairman Joe Mears.

My father was very proud of what I'd helped achieve at Chelsea and the acknowledgment and respect you receive from other players who appreciate the significance of winning the First Division title made it even more special. Manchester City's centre-half, David Ewing, and Burnley's Doug Winton were both good friends of mine and we had a bigger celebration together during the summer of 1955 than anything arranged by Chelsea.

As a professional footballer you are always striving to get to the top and compete with the best, so to have achieved something so significant for Chelsea Football club was something else. Winning that medal at Stamford Bridge made me so proud.

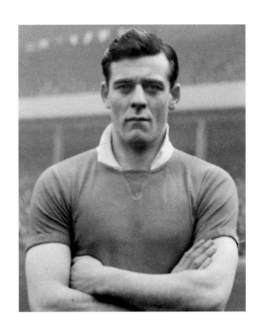

Peter
Sillett

The Sillett brothers, John [left] & Peter [right] on the pitch at Stamford Bridge

Peter Sillett scoring his critical penalty in the title clincher against Wolves

Peter was a giant of a man, both in size and performance. My abiding memory of him is his penalty against Wolves on the Easter Saturday of the Championship year. Chelsea needed to beat Wolves if they were to go on and clinch the title. Stamford Bridge was absolutely packed and the gates had to be shut an hour before kick-off.

Seamus O'Connell had a goal-bound shot handled by Wolves' Billy Wright. At first the referee failed to spot the incident, but after talking to his linesman, Peter Sillett had to face the most pressurised kick of his career. Penalty kicks were food and drink to Peter, but this one was so important. He put the ball on the spot and absolutely belted it.

Peter, like Ted Drake, started his career at Southampton. Peter's brother John was also at Chelsea and they became an unusual combination as full-backs at Stamford Bridge. *Albert Sewell*

Jim
Lewis

England amateur internation Captain, Jim Lewis, introduces Field Marshal Montgomery

1952 — Jim Lewis during Walthamstow's Cup replay with Manchester United at Highbury

Because my Dad had been such a loyal Walthamstow Avenue player, I suppose it was inevitable that I would end up at the same club, so after progressing through the schoolboy set-up, I eventually broke into their first team when I was sixteen. My father, Jim Lewis (Senior), was still in the side at that stage and having such a close ally as a teammate was a unique situation. Dad was a good wing-half and won an amateur international cap. It would be fair to say, though, that my Mum was just as big an influence on my career as anyone else, she was heavily involved with Walthamstow too. I considered myself to be a straightforward player, possessing pace and the ability to score goals rather than being full of tricks and creativity, but I did have moments when I did like to dribble and take people on. In fact Tony Banks, the MP, once told me that his first memory of watching me at Stamford Bridge was taking the ball round two or three players, so perhaps some of the fans saw me in a different light to the one I did.

I was then whisked away to India with the Army to do my National Service, where I played a lot of football against some very good sides, including one very impressive outfit from Calcutta by the name of Mohan Bagan while I was over there. I remember our regiment side competing in the India Cup, which was a competition that was held in Bombay and attracted the best sides from all over the country. In one of the cup games we were playing one of the stands collapsed and the match was cancelled. There weren't any fatalities, but it was terrible to witness and a lot of people were injured - that was the last year that the competition was held.

After the Army I returned to playing for The Avenue, who seemed to be improving all the time, culminating in a great FA Cup run in 1952 where we beat Wimbledon three-nil, Watford two-one and Stockport two-one, before being pulled out of the hat with Manchester United at Old Trafford. I scored up there in a one-all draw which meant United had to come to London for a replay, but for obvious reasons the fixture was switched to Highbury so that we could get a decent sized crowd for the game. I scored another two in the replay, but unfortunately we went down five-two, although the margin could have been a lot closer because Trevor Bailey, an England cricketer at the time, missed an absolute sitter right near the end, hitting the crossbar from about a yard out.

Walthamstow used to get between seven and a half and fifteen thousand fans for the bigger games and the stadium had one large stand which also housed a ballroom, a stage, a big bar, snooker tables, and underneath that lot, a shooting range. Today, Walthamstow is sadly no more, the Greenpond Road ground has been sold off and the club doesn't exist, which is a great shame. Their last game was in 1988 before merging with Leytonstone and more recently merged again to become Dagenham and Redbridge.

After that game against Manchester United a lot of people started to wonder why I hadn't been offered a full time professional contract before. I did have a brief spell at Leyton Orient, and had signed amateur forms for West Ham, but neither worked out for me. On reflection, looking back at my time at Brisbane Road, I think I found it easier to score goals in the First Division than I did in the Third Division South! Charlton also offered me a contract, but the wages were so low that I had to say no.

Walthamstow's great Cup run changed things for me and Ted Drake was on the phone within twenty-four hours of our elimination to see if I would like to join Chelsea - which I did. Ted was the main factor in me going to Stamford Bridge, as a forward I was keen to learn from a man who had been of the highest calibre during his own career. The only other London club I may have considered at the time was Tottenham, but my mother disliked Spurs and my family would be very upset if I'd joined them.

My first two games for Chelsea were both against Charlton at The Valley, the first was a reserve game in midweek, then I went into the first team for a memorable return trip the following Saturday where I scored on my full debut and got off to the best possible start. I'll always remember the amount of people inside the ground that afternoon and the vast terrace, it was an imposing setting for a debut I thought. The crowds back in those days always seemed so impressive and whenever I show people my playing-day photographs, they're always fascinated by the huge numbers of people that were crammed into the stadiums back then. I scored four goals in my first nine games for Chelsea, including strikes against Tottenham, Liverpool and Manchester City, but scoring against Spurs was the highlight for me because I'd grown up in that neck of the woods.

I also remember my first hat trick for Chelsea, against Portsmouth in the four-three win in August 1953, I missed a penalty in that game too! I recall a feeling of satisfaction rather than elation in scoring those three goals because as an amateur player, surrounded by professionals, it was important to prove I was up to the job and deserved to be selected on merit. At the end of the day I had another job, but it was my teammate's living, so I had to pull my weight. The other players were great though, there was never any animosity and I never felt an outsider even though I didn't train with them every day. I also had a good relationship with the Chelsea fans and they were always very generous to me. I always tried to give 100% and I think people recognised that.

September 1954 — Jim Lewis wins a header against Preston North End during a 1–0 defeat

Jim Lewis is beaten to the ball by the Sheffield Wednesday 'keeper

Jim Lewis heads home past Manchester City's goalie, Burt Trautmann

One of the things that struck me about the professional players was, compared to the amateurs I'd played with previously, was that before a big game they always weighed up their chances, and when travelling up to play at certain grounds, they seemed almost superstitious about how 'lucky' and 'unlucky' certain stadiums were. At Walthamstow, everywhere we went we approached the game as if we would win it, no matter where we played. I appreciate some grounds were fairly intimidating, places like Liverpool where our coach got stoned, but Chelsea had a very good team and there should have been no reason to question why, "we'll be lucky to get a point up there".

I could understand why opposing teams always fancied their chances when they came to The Bridge though, that huge dog track round the edge of the pitch really distanced the players from the atmosphere the crowd generated. Another factor was that because the home fans were so generous with their appreciation of good play, from either side, things were made too easy for visitors. I doubt that's the case today.

Some people can't understand, even when Chelsea signed me, why I never gave up my career as a travelling salesman, but the simple fact of the matter was that with the maximum wage rule in place, I was able to earn more in business than I could from football. In the early Fifties footballers were still considered well paid for what they did, but workers were still able to match footballer's earnings if they were reasonably successful in a more traditional line of work. That seems unbelievable today when you read what the current Chelsea first-teamers take home every week.

My company was very good to me too, I was allowed as much time off work to play the game as I needed, which included lots of overseas trips with London and England amateurs, and ultimately, the Great Britain Olympic football team. I was fortunate to represent my country forty-nine times and travelled with Great Britain to the 1952 Games in Helsinki, Melbourne in 1956, and then Rome in 1960. I was also invited out to play in Tom Finney's tour side, along with the likes of Bobby Moore, travelling to the Far East and New Zealand. Through playing football I got to travel to almost every corner of the globe. Training was a bit of a problem though, so my personal regime was very unconventional, not that I was too keen on it in any case.

Because my job took me all over the country during the week, I had an arrangement with several clubs around England where I could just turn up and train... places like Grimsby! Looking back I don't regret a thing and I'm sure that I made the right decisions because after football I was able to progress up the career ladder further than I would have done if I'd entered my trade later in life. Before I retired, I was national sales manager for my company. The downside, though, was having two bosses to keep happy instead of one!

Probably the most memorable game from the Championship season, and the game that a lot of fans still talk about today, was the five-six defeat to Manchester United at Stamford Bridge. Any Chelsea supporter listening out for the result on the radio after the match must have assumed their team had won when the first part of the score was read out! From my perspective, though, what I remember most vividly, is the fact that of the five goals Chelsea scored, the amateurs scored four. I got one and Seamus O'Connell got three.

Seamus was a real rogue, a very successful man with the ladies! Believe it or not, despite his name, he played for England at amateur level and we used to room together on tours. I remember in Bulgaria, I woke up one morning to find he'd been out in the street bartering and sold the last of my new nylon shirts. They had just come out in England and were very in vogue, so over in Sofia they were like gold dust. He'd sold three for a big bundle of Bulgarian bank notes, that was before we learned that the money was useless outside the country, so we blew the lot on wooden ornaments as gifts for people back home. There's not much to buy in Sofia. It was like being a film star over there, ours was one of the first western sides to visit for donkey's years and there were crowds of people outside our hotel every day. I think I got to know Seamus better than anyone at Chelsea.

I was used in several positions at Chelsea, mainly at outside-right, whereas for England and Walthamstow I'd always been a centre-forward or pushed to outside-right. I was in and out of the side like a yo-yo and the number of times I was named as twelfth man was amazing. I felt no bitterness towards any of the players who were keeping me out, everyone got on and I considered them all my friends.

In those days, with no substitutes, if you were named as twelfth man, unless one of your team-mates dropped dead before the game started, you simply didn't play at all. Looking back it doesn't seem that long ago when injured players simply had to leave the field without being replaced, the team just had to continue with ten men, which seems ridiculous. Because there was no chance of being replaced, so many players were forced to carry on playing in matches, and in doing so, made injuries ten times worse. That's just how things were back then.

Travelling with the side, then not playing, didn't upset me too much I don't think, I'd have rather played, naturally, but I still felt involved and at least I learned how to play Brag! Ken Armstrong, Stan Willemse and Bobby Smith ran the Chelsea card school, and as an unsuspecting amateur, I ended up writing a cheque to one of them on my first away trip. Ken Armstrong had an almost photographic memory and he used to make a lot of money out of the lads, until The Gaffer stopped it. Losing a bundle before a game became a distraction to some players believe it or not!

It was just a shame that there were no subs back then because I could have been used in any of the attacking positions and these days I'm sure I would have been brought on in most games during the course of the season and would have scored more goals for Chelsea. I got to spend a lot of time with Ted Drake and Jack Oxberry on the sidelines though, which was an education, and it was clear that Ted kicked every shot and headed every ball, he was so engrossed in the games. One of the funniest things I ever saw at Chelsea happened in those circumstances, Ted jumped up to 'nod in' a cross but forgot he was inside the dugout, he smashed his head so hard on the concrete roof that I thought he had knocked himself out. Jack and myself had to bite our tongues, but I'll always remember that moment.

Jack Oxberry was a very quiet man, he always struck me as being a country man stuck in the city. He was a very slow, deliberate speaker and very calm with it. Unlike Ted, I never saw Jack lose his temper. Ted was a funny old bugger at times, he'd shout at you when you didn't stand an earthly chance of being able to have done what he expected. I remember being given a right rollicking during one game for not intercepting a ball that I would have had to have been a bolt of lightning to have caught – I was fast, but not that fast!

I did consider myself pretty quick back then, my pace often allowed me to nip in and shoot, in fact I was nearly as fast as Eric Parsons and he was known as 'Rabbit'. Speed-wise, neither of us were in the same class as people like Thierry Henry or Michael Owen, not by a long way, some of these modern day players are like greyhounds. To be totally honest, I feel our modern day counterparts have got so much more ability and skill than we did too, I really do, but the balls have probably got something to do with it. It was difficult being an artisan when the rock-hard ball was caked in mud and weighed a ton.

I started the Championship season well, missing just one of the first sixteen matches, and until Frank Blunstone's return from injury, I'd enjoyed my longest run in the side since arriving. Being on the sidelines and witnessing the season hotting up was tremendously exciting, but very frustrating at the same time. I could sense that the Championship was Chelsea's, even though inwardly I didn't believe we'd ever finish top, I just couldn't picture it in my head. But I suppose, looking back, I could be a little bit more dispassionate about the whole Championship issue, I wasn't a professional, my livelihood wasn't at stake.

Playing in the same team as Roy Bentley was another attraction for me, he was a great striker. Roy was also a tremendous person and in my opinion he was the best player in that side - without any doubt. In fact I'd go as far as to say that I doubt anyone could have a bad word to say about Roy, well, nobody who was on the same team as he was anyway, he was a hard man to play against. I admit that hard men were two-a-penny back then, but Roy had something extra to his game, something special. Talking about getting clattered, I'm not lying when I say that I'm still limping from an injury one notorious defender inflicted. He was one of the few players to have a go to my face about amateur players keeping decent players out of the game, I remember telling him to ease off and keep his views to himself. Then he warned me that if I thought I would finish the game, I was very much mistaken - with about five minutes to go he got me, I was out for almost a month.

That was just part of the game though and Ted Drake was as guilty as anyone in enforcing hard tactics. He would prime John Harris before the game regarding who to single out. In the team-talk before our game up at Newcastle the Gaffer told John not to let Bobby Mitchell get past him more than twice, if he did, to kick him up in the air and make sure it didn't happen a third time. Poor Bobby was sent sprawling after about ten minutes and we didn't see much of him again that afternoon.

Looking back at when Chelsea actually clinched the title in their final home game, it strikes me that absolutely no thought and little preparation had been put into anything whatsoever. The club knew how close they were to clinching the biggest prize in it's history, yet no celebrations were planned which seems remarkable. Nothing, not even on the off chance, had been considered, not even a single bottle of champagne! I realise things were different back then, people celebrated differently, including the players, you only have to look at footage of goals being scored from that era, but to have overlooked such an obvious chance to celebrate after waiting so long to win something seems ridiculous.

Looking back at the old photos of the winning squad assembled in the stand after the final whistle against Sheffield Wednesday still makes me laugh, the scruffy old tracksuits look terrible. I'm sure the other players have told you about their 'special' Championship prize suits, but as an amateur I wasn't even allowed to receive one of those, they were the rules - no payment for playing and no bonuses, which the suit was classed as. My reward was far more special in hindsight, I was presented with an Illuminated Address, a hand painted, framed scroll with my name on, recording the achievement. Unfortunately my wife didn't like me putting my football memorabilia and photographs up in the living room so for the last fifty years it's had to hang in my toilet!

1955 — Jim Lewis receives his Illuminated Address for his part in Chelsea's Championship

Jim Lewis scores from close range in front of an impressive crowd

My record as a footballer is one I am very proud of - five hundred and six goals in six hundred and seventy-three games. I played five hundred and twenty-two games for Walthamstow and scored four hundred and twenty-three goals. For Chelsea; forty goals in ninety-five games, England amateurs; thirty-nine goals in forty-nine games and for the Great Britain Olympic team, four goals in seven matches... Don't ask me to remember them all though!

The Championship certainly doesn't feel half a century ago, sometimes I think to myself 'that can't be fifty years, I'm not really that old am I?', then I realise it was and I am. When the team had its first reunion, at the House of Commons in 1999, I was also shocked how hard it was to recognise some of my old team-mates, getting old is a terrible business. I've only been back to Stamford Bridge a handful of times since leaving in 1958, but everything was so different now. The lovely ivy on the offices has disappeared and the players' snooker room has vanished, but, even at the expense of a lot of the character, the stadium is very impressive.

As a striker, as well as the memorable goals, it's inevitable that you have memorable misses too and the one that still makes me cringe from my time at Chelsea came in the FA Cup in 1958. We were playing Darlington in the Fourth Round and amazingly found ourselves three goals down at half time, but we came back in the second half to take the match to a replay. We went up to their mud-heap for the return and with the score at one-all and time running out, I missed from a yard out. The match went to extra time and they scored three goals to knock us out. It's a long way back from Darlington when you lose, and on top of that, I was dropped for a few matches following the Cup exit.

An altogether far better trip I recall was travelling over with Chelsea for a tour of the States. Ted rang up my Managing Director at work and cleared it for me to fly out with the team and we played a series of matches with Glasgow Rangers, Fortuna Dusseldorf and Burussia Dortmund, against American 'All Star' teams to an audience of what I guess were largely ex-patriots Europeans at Baseball stadiums. The crowds were small but some of the games were high scoring, so there must have been some entertainment value.

There was plenty of free time though and I remember the squad getting invited to the races as a guest of one of the track owners over there. He greeted us on our arrival and made us feel very welcome, then, after speaking to us for a while, he said, "by the way guys, Go West in fourth", before walking off to sort a problem out. After looking through the race card and seeing the horse listed, we decided to put our money on it. The animal came out of the traps and didn't stop accelerating, winning by about ten lengths. We had a good day and had all won a lot of money, so in the last race we decided we'd pool our syndicate winnings, but we eventually lost the lot on a photo finish!

The Chairman, Joe Mears and his ex-showgirl wife were on the tour with us in America, and because she used to work in the theatre and had contacts in the States, we all got invited to see a Burlesque show in New Jersey. It was thought that the players should attend the show to help promote our tour matches, but the funny thing was, after about twenty minutes, all the players got ushered out of the theatre and told to leave because the Chairman had decided what we were watching was too risqué and not suitable for young players to be watching. They didn't realise there was nudity in this particular variety show, but to this day, I have no idea what Chelsea and Rangers were doing over there in the first place!

Stan
Wicks

1955 – Peter Sillett & Stan Wicks are beaten to the ball by Arsenal's Tommy Lawton

Stan Wicks poses for a photograph before his Chelsea debut

Ted Drake knew all about Stan because he managed the player at Reading, so it wasn't a big surprise that they teamed up again at Chelsea. Stan's arrival at Stamford Bridge is often seen as the signing that turned Chelsea from contenders into Champions. He was a big, tall central defender who was incredibly strong in the air - and when crosses came in fans could almost look away and relax because Wicks was so dependable. A great signing. Unfortunately injury cut short his playing career, then more tragically, Stan lost a brave fight with cancer in February 1983. *Albert Sewell*

Eric
Parsons

Eric Parsons [second from right] in the West Ham dressing room with his team-mates

1952 – Parsons goes up with Burnley's goalie at Turf Moor

My nickname, "Rabbit", started at West Ham, not because of the amount of talking I did, but because I used to run in fits and starts and was pretty quick on grass. My natural speed is something that I've always relied on, even from knee-high - I was champion of the school and my athletics club as well as 220-yard champion of Sussex - speed was something that I was just born with. It was the fans who started calling me the name first, you used to get a lot of humour from the crowds in the East End and I had a lot of good times at West Ham. I went there as a schoolboy after impressing in a Sussex Boys game against The Hammers, joining them straight from school at fifteen as part of the ground staff at first.

When the War broke out I left London straight away, I was in digs in East Ham and wanted to get back to Worthing where I've lived all my life. I got called up when I was eighteen and joined the Army and served with the Desert Rats, but my football developed while I was in service and I ended up playing with the British Army of the Rhine. There were some very good players in that team, including big Les Compton - that was a good time for me. I was in the Forces for five years until I was demobbed in 1947 when I returned to West Ham. My professional career took off then and I made a name for myself in the first team, then Chelsea came in for me and I was transferred in 1950.

There are only two players who played in every match during the Championship season, and I'm proud to say that I am one of them! Myself and Derek Saunders are unique in that respect and we can both look back and say that we didn't miss a kick during the club's finest ever season. They were lovely days at Chelsea.

I was already at Chelsea when Ted Drake arrived, I'd been signed by the previous manager, Billy Birrell, but when the new Gaffer came in I was struggling for fitness after right knee troubles which resulted in a cartilage and ligament operation.

Ted Drake was a far more knowledgeable manager than Billy Birrell, especially from a player's point of view. The medical treatment I received from the club was first rate I thought, and thankfully I was able to play as good football when I'd got back to fitness as I was playing before I got crocked. The knee gives me a lot of gip now though and I walk with a bit of a limp, but I suppose at seventy-eight I'm entitled to that after all the running I've done in my time!

My confidence was a bit down though when I was recovering and I remember Ted Drake giving me a big boost with some of the things he said in the press. I'd always admired Drake as a player, he was a bustling centre-forward who never seemed to struggle to find the net, but he went up in my estimation by some of the things he said as my manager.

Ted told the 'papers that if the club showed faith in me and allowed me time to recover properly he was sure that I'd return the faith and give my all for the club - which is what I did I think. I was determined to get back to my best, it was hard work I recall, but I always trained hard and came through it. Knee operations were a bit dodgy in those days, you could never be too sure that you'd ever return to how things were, but Chelsea gave me every possible assistance.

Because Ted was such a prolific striker with Arsenal, he would come and have a word in my ear from time to time to help me improve my shooting or finishing, or about what he wanted extra from me. Ted's team-talks were always pretty good, he wound us up a bit before the game and if you weren't doing what he wanted. At half-time he'd have a right go at you - there could be an awful lot of shouting going on in the dressing room if things weren't going our way.

I scored a fair few goals in that Championship season I know, but it's such a shame that it seems an awfully long time ago now and unfortunately my memory isn't what it was so it's hard to recall the goals, even the ones that helped clinch the title. I do remember the crowds though, what tremendous support the Chelsea fans gave us, there were so many people inside Stamford Bridge every match day that they had to lock people out quite frequently and to play in front of seventy thousand fans became almost normal. There was a huge bank on one side of the ground, which looked fantastic as I was running down the wing. Unfortunately, when you're playing centre stage, you have to concentrate so much on the game itself and making sure you're switched on to your team-mates, that you don't get the chance to absorb the atmosphere that a crowd of that size generates.

I used to commute from Worthing to London every day, catching the eight o'clock train in the morning and returning back from Victoria at around two in the afternoon. My team-mates, Stan Willemse, who'd played in the same Sussex schoolboys team as me, and John McNichol, used to travel in with me some mornings, as they were both based in Brighton, but most mornings I'd be accompanied by my neighbour Jimmy. The train would get into London at twenty past nine, as regular as clockwork, it was a great service and I could rely on getting into training on time for our ten o'clock start, so there was no reason to move any nearer.

I thrived on training, I absolutely loved it. I could run and run and run and the harder they made it the more I enjoyed myself, it was great for building up stamina. We'd start by going out for a long run, every player at the club, and get back after about an hour and do a lot of sprint exercises, which was really my cup of tea. Frank Blunstone was

1954 – Rabbit poses with a new delivery of footballs at Stamford Bridge

March 1955 – Parsons misses out to Aston Villa's 'keeper, Jones, in a 3-2 defeat at Villa Park

April 1955 – Eric Parsons heads home past Sheffield Wednesday's goalie, McIntosh

quick, but he was the only one who'd get close to me, not that Frank used to get that near! I remember turning round to Frankie in training and egging him on; "come on, come on, get a bit closer to me" I used to shout, and I'm sure that helped him to get even quicker. He'd never have caught me though! Frank was a lovely lad, the baby of the team, but he added so much when he arrived and made his mark on the first team - he was one of those players that helped turn us into real title contenders. Ted was no mug, he knew how to spot a good player, he was always on the look out for ways of tweaking the side.

Some people have asked me in the past whether, if I had my time again, I would have gone into athletics rather than football, but I loved the game so much that there's no way I would want to miss the experience. I consider football players as athletes in any case, in fact there is probably more skill and ability involved in a team sport, running is one thing, but if you can't control a ball or know what to do with it, all you're good at is just running. But saying that, a lot of the football I watch on television today, I just turn off. To my mind a lot of players simply do the wrong thing and don't take players on any more - there's certainly not enough wing-play. I'd even go as far as to say that a lot of today's top players aren't really that good at all and the money they earn is ridiculous. I used to think 'good luck to them', but it's got out of control now.

Myself and Johnny McNichol formed a good partnership on that right flank for Chelsea, he was a good passer of the ball and he would thread them through and send me away and we were both very much on the same wavelength. We got on well off the pitch too.

Our Chelsea side was an extremely good one in my opinion, to win the title was something I never felt I'd be part of, but through hard graft and a tough, workman like attitude we pulled off something that the club has only achieved once in it's history. I always dreamed about winning, every player does I expect, but only a handful of players are lucky enough to win a Championship medal. You sometimes wonder if you'll be one of the lucky ones. I know one or two of my Chelsea team-mates have had to sell their winners' medals in recent years, but that's something I could never do, I know I'd regret it for the rest of my life.

With players like Stan Willemse, Ken Armstrong, John Harris, Roy Bentley and Stan Wicks, few opposing teams were going to intimidate us and a few of the lads were rewarded by being called up for England because of the team's success. I was playing at my best in 1954-55, there's no doubt about that, so perhaps I deserved a full cap that season as well. I did have the honour to play for England B though and felt I played well too, but that's the nearest I got unfortunately.

January 1955 — Eric Parsons and Les Stubbs in action in the Cup tie at Bristol Rovers

1955 — Eric Parsons waiting to pounce as Roy Bentley is beaten to the ball

I moved on to Brentford after Chelsea and had four good years at Griffin Park after winning the First Division Championship in 1955. I played a lot of games for Brentford, but then again I played a lot of games! I thrived on running and playing football.

I didn't want to carry on in the game as a coach or become a manager when I'd hung my boots up, all that travelling over the years was hard work and I couldn't face it if I wasn't playing. So I decided to fend for myself away from the game, firstly I ran a grocer's shop, then I started a cigarette vending business which grew and grew and it became very successful indeed and really set me up. Today I still live in Worthing with my wife and we've got a nice flat overlooking the sea.

I must admit that the Championship win seems an awfully long time ago now and I can't believe, even after all these years, Chelsea have never matched our success. Still, I wish them well, I had a wonderful time at Stamford Bridge and I hope the fans get another set of Champions to celebrate soon.

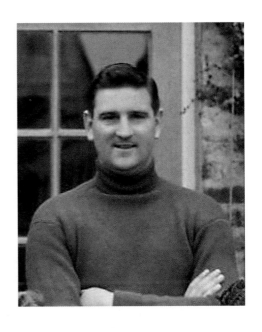

Bill
Robertson

September 1954 — Bill Robertson airbourne during The Blues' 2-1 win at Sheffield United

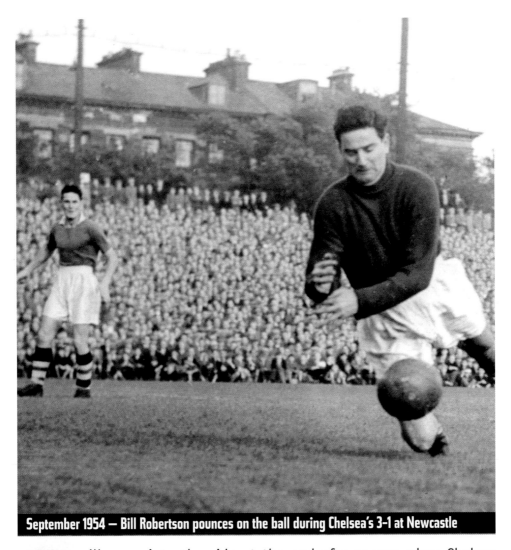

September 1954 — Bill Robertson pounces on the ball during Chelsea's 3-1 at Newcastle

Bill came into the side at the end of a season when Chelsea were threatened with relegation, in fact they survived only on goal average after winning the last four games. Robertson was a big, broad-boned Scot but he was a bundle of nerves off the pitch. Before a match he would be pacing up and down, smoking away and the players used to say that he went onto the field like a jelly. On his debut the trainer had to administer a couple of stiff whiskeys to calm him down.

But once the game got going he changed and was a rock at the back. Although Bill never really became the most established of 'keepers at Stamford Bridge, his saves played a big part in allowing the Championship challenge to become possible. If Chelsea had been relegated in 1951, history could have been so different.

Bill died in 1973 aged forty-four. *Albert Sewell*

Derek
Saunders

I was born in Ware in Hertfordshire and only really got into playing football because I was persuaded to join a local youth centre. The man who set the club up gave all the children who joined a new sense of responsibility and we built up a great sense of camaraderie, before long we'd established a very good football team and had started to do very well. I also learned how to box and dance at the club. We had a really marvellous team of fifteen and sixteen-year-olds, so good in fact that before long our team was asked to become Ware Town and join the Isthmian League.

Unlike most boys of my age I didn't have to join up with the Forces during the War or do National Service because of my job, I worked repairing tractors and farm equipment, which was considered essential work. I had tried office work but hated it, I walked out after about six weeks because I thought it was so dull.

Because our side were continuing to progress and I was developing as a player, my uncle said he would try and get me a trial at Millwall. He worked on the canals and took his barge up to Millwall Docks a lot and he had a few contacts within the football club. I remember going up to the ground and walking out of the tube station just as a huge bomb landed about three hundred yards up the road which sent a big cloud of rubbish up in the air.

Despite the bad omen of the blast things went quite well and I was asked to play in a couple of matches for them at inside-forward and I scored a goal before being dropped. I lost interest in Millwall after that and decided to join Walthamstow Avenue and was in the same team as Jim Lewis' father. A couple of years afterwards, Freddie Cox, an ex-Arsenal player, came in as coach and he had a huge influence on me as a player. After watching me play for a few games he gave some advice I will never forget, he told me; "stop doing every other bugger's work and do your own." So that's what I started to do, I stopped charging up and down the pitch trying to take everyone on and covering for everyone else and concentrated on my own position and my game came on leaps and bounds. Within six months I'd been picked to represent England at amateur level and played five games for my country including one, against France, as captain. I was also asked to play for Middlesex Wanderers, an amateur budding-youngsters team that toured Europe playing in exhibition and charity matches.

Amateur football was very big back then and there were some excellent footballers at that level. Because of the maximum wage many players chose to stay in their jobs because they could earn as much as a professional and have more security, so the amateur leagues were every bit as strong as the lower divisions, if not better in some cases.

1952 – Derek Saunders and his Walthamstow team-mates lift the Amateur Cup at Wembley

1952 — Derek Saunders leads the Walthamstow lads out before a full house at Wembley

Jim Lewis & Derek Saunders — Team mates at Walthamstow, Champions at Chelsea

I was also picked to play for Great Britain in the 1952 Olympic Games in Helsinki. We lost three-one to Hungary in the first stages and I was so upset that I remember leaving the field in tears - I was so emotional that the Italian referee came over and tried to console me.

Walthamstow fought through to the Amateur Cup Final in 1952 too, so on top of all the high profile games I was playing in, I was beginning to get noticed by several professional teams, including Southend United, Arsenal, and of course, Chelsea. I must say that the deciding factor in leaving Walthamstow was definitely Ted Drake though, he called to ask if he could visit me at home, and after meeting the man, my mind was made up. Ted was the kind of person I felt at ease with, he was easy to talk to, reasonable and I felt he really wanted me at the club. He spoke about me coming into the team and helping to shore up the defence, he said he was impressed about how I read the game and how I intercepted, covered and tackled. The only problem I had about signing there and then was that I was about to go on holiday to the South of France for three weeks and I didn't want to lose the money I'd paid out. Ted didn't see this as a problem, in fact, he even agreed to pay for the trip if I signed and met up with the rest of the squad for training when I got back, so I had a free holiday on Chelsea - which was nice. Being at Stamford Bridge was out of this world, the atmosphere among the players and supporters was fantastic.

I didn't sign as a professional with Chelsea straight away, but Ted persuaded me to pack my job in after a few months and it proved to be one of the best things I've ever done in my life. My game improved dramatically because of what I learnt from the other players as well as my knowledge of the game. I learnt that if you pushed the ball to one player, then ran into an open space, you didn't always get the ball back because there was so much more ability surrounding me, to go into a side with players like Johnny McNichol and Eric Parsons was so special. Ron Greenwood was also very good to me, he coached me too and helped me when I first arrived. He was a very gentle man, he wouldn't say a word out of place, very mild mannered.

They were all such a nice bunch, all of them, which went a long way to winning the title I think. Everyone got on and wanted to work for each other on the pitch, if somebody made a mistake we still called them a right so-and-so but did everything we could to get back and help them make amends. Having big Stan Willemse behind me on the field was a great fail-safe though, if anyone got past me, I knew they certainly wouldn't get past him too. Some people say that I wasn't shy of dishing it out on the pitch, which I suppose is a fair thing to say, but whereas some players would take the man instead of the ball, I felt I

Derek Saunders [second left] dress up in Holland with the Middlesex Wanderers

August 1959 — Saunders [middle] poses with the team flying out to Ajax of Amsterdam

always took the ball first, then the man. I only ever got booked once in my whole career though, but that probably says more about how rough the game was rather than my impeccable discipline.

I used to be able to look after myself on the pitch, I never shirked out of a tackle, but I would never go looking for trouble, I used to stick close to my opponent from the start and make sure he didn't get the ball in the first ten minutes - if I managed that they were sure to have a stinker. If I was going to make a tackle I was damned sure I was going to win that ball, there was no two ways about it. The only time I can remember going after somebody was during the four-three win at Wolves during the Championship season, one of their players clattered into me from behind and I went down like an ox. There was a bit of a scuffle, Roy Bentley came back and was pushing this guy around, then I got up and thought about really walloping him, the red mist had come down, but fortunately I pulled back as I knew I'd get sent off.

There was always a lot of needle in those games against Wolves and myself and Bill Slater, their inside-forward, always had a real battle. Neither of us would back out of a challenge and neither of us were prepared to give an inch. The season before we'd lost eight-one at Molineux, but we were only playing with ten men because we'd lost our centre-half and there were no substitutes. I was shifted to the centre of the defence, every damn ball was then played down the middle and I had the busiest afternoon of my career. I'll never forget that game.

I also remember one of my team-mates stepping in to help me out away at Cardiff, just after I'd arrived at Chelsea. I was having a rough old time against their centre-forward who knocked me for six every time I went up to head a ball. Johnny Harris came over in the end and said, "next time, leave him to me...", so I did. The next minute the guy was flat out on the floor, felled by a head-butt to the back of the neck - 'Gentleman John' had struck!

Ted was chopping and changing the team quite a bit in the season before the Championship campaign and it wasn't until after Christmas that things started to settle down and a more established team started to emerge. I was delighted to be part of the core squad and to finish eighth in the League, and to know that I would be in the team at the start of the following season was a great feeling for me personally. Ted gave us all such a gee-up during pre-season training that summer so we were all fired up when the first game arrived. I know every manager does the same with their squad, but added to the fact that the team were now more settled and confident than ever, there was a belief, especially in me, that we were able to achieve something special in 1954-55. We all admired Ted Drake and if he believed it, then so did we.

September 1954 — Saunders, Parsons & Greenwood defend during 3-1 win at Newcastle

Derek Saunders [in white] in the middle of the action in an away game at Everton

To me the Championship season really ebbed and flowed, things were never really going badly that season and there was a belief in the squad, then when we moved into fourth place I knew we'd win the title. My personal form during that season was as I'd hoped, and because some of my team-mates were being called up to represent England, I hoped and I prayed that my turn would come too, but it wasn't to be. I wasn't one to seek attention, I never felt comfortable in the limelight, but to have represented my country as a full international would have been a tremendous honour - but I tried hard.

One of the things I am extremely proud of from the Championship season is the fact that along with Eric Parsons, I didn't miss a single match, which is a hard thing to achieve, believe me! There were a few times that we both hid injuries so we didn't miss matches. Eric struggled on with a dodgy ankle on two or three occasions and I gashed my shin badly tripping over a metal post in training on a Friday afternoon which I was able to battle on with, even though it needed stitches. I played the next day and had quite a good game, but I've still got a scar all the way down my leg.

Ken Armstrong was my counterpart on the right-hand side of the pitch and was a daintier player, he was slightly more attack-minded than myself perhaps and would make himself available for passes more often. But Ted always used to tell me to "stick like glue" to whoever I was marking, and to do that, it meant I had to hold my position and not venture too far forward unless we were really chasing a game. Because I rarely crossed the half-way line I only scored a handful of goals for Chelsea. I often remember the one I scored at Tottenham in 1957, I smashed it from about thirty-five yards and the Spurs 'keeper, Ted Ditchburn, just stood planted to the spot as the ball went in the top corner of the net.

Another memorable goal was at Bolton Wanderers who were playing the offside trap all the time, so it was decided that I should surprise the opposition and make a late run forward and the ball would be played over the top for me to run on to. It worked a treat and there I was, alone up front, to head the ball over the stranded goalie who had come out of his area to try and intercept the ball. I got one in the Championship season too, away at West Brom - we were two-nil down with about twenty minutes to go and I decided to let fly again and fortunately helped Chelsea get back into a game we went on to win four-two.

I think the best inside-forward I had to mark was Burnley's Irish International, Jimmy McIlroy, he was very useful and always gave me plenty of stick - it struck me that he was a player with a similar outlook to me. There used to be a wall about three feet high behind the goal up at Burnley, and one match we had a right ding-dong and I ended up over the top of it following a corner. He didn't foul me, but after running in at goal from about twenty yards out we collided in the air going up for the header, then bang! I don't know where the ball went, but I went over the top of the wall and was fortunate that the ground was full, otherwise I'd have ended up a crumpled mess on the concrete terracing. I hated going to Burnley.

Ted was a good tactician I thought, the only times I can really remember him being out-foxed was when Don Revie brought his Manchester City side to Stamford Bridge and played a 4-2-4 which we really struggled to fathom out and were two-nil down at half-time. We changed things around at the break but the score didn't change. The other game, of course, was the five-six defeat to Manchester United, but I thought that was a lovely, lovely game to be involved with despite the score. I remember myself and Stan Willemse were at fault for a couple of those goals, we got our marking mixed up at two corners where we thought we knew best, but there was an amazing finale to the match and we never stopped chasing the game.

Apart from winning my Championship medal, I think my personal highlight from my time at the club happened up at Bolton, playing against the great man, Nat Lofthouse and he'd given me the run-around all afternoon. Then, later on in the game, I saw him running at me again, and I was able to nip in and win the ball off him, I laid it off and set off into space and looked up for the return ball, which came straight at my feet. As I crossed the half-way line it seemed as if everything just opened up, the centre-half came to tackle me so I dropped my shoulder and he went the wrong way - then I buried the ball past the goalie to score a goal I'll never forget. That was the nicest feeling I ever experienced in football, everything I did worked perfectly, to run the whole length of the field, then score was a fabulous experience.

Our tours abroad with Chelsea were always memorable too, especially the trip to America and Canada in May 1954. I was known as 'Blood Saunders' in the newspapers over in the States, because of my head of bright red hair which was always a bit wild and up in the air. The football was easy over there, we were winning comfortably in most games, until we travelled up to Toronto to play Glasgow Rangers when obviously the opposition was stronger. We played Rangers three times, losing one-nil, winning four-one and drawing nil-nil, but it was an amazing trip and I've got some great memories of visiting Niagara Falls with all the Chelsea boys.

Travelling to away games with Chelsea was a good way of getting to know the supporters in those days - we often all used to share the same

Saunders talks tactics before a game against Manchester United

train going up and down the country. The players would always have their own carriage, but the fans would pass through and come and speak to us which was a good way of relaxing and socialising. Ted would buy the players a pint in the buffet bar on the way back if we'd won, just the one drink mind, but there were no crates of brown ale being passed back down the train from the fans to us or anything like that!

Chelsea have always enjoyed great away support, even in the days when it was more difficult to get around the country. For the longer distance games we'd always stay in a top hotel the night before. The atmosphere at Stamford Bridge, especially in the big games, was always tremendous too, as the crowd filled the stadium the noise would filter down on top of you and the vast banks of fans looked a fantastic sight.

After the low-key Championship celebrations, the team went away for a tour and as a surprise all the wives were flown out to Paris for the weekend to join us - which turned out to be quite eventful. Harry Green, Chelsea's assistant secretary, had made all the transport arrangements for the ladies, but the wrong time had been printed on all the plane tickets and they missed the flight from Heathrow. Because there was only one flight a day back then, and to save the day, Harry took it upon himself to charter a private Dove aeroplane from Croydon Airport and fly them out from there. My personal reward for playing in every match that season, was a £1 per game bonus, I was given a cheque for £42.

But that trip to France was Chelsea's only European campaign as Champions, as for some reason, despite winning the First Division title, we were never entered for European competition, which looking back is baffling because Chelsea were invited to enter the inaugural European Cup but withdrew their entry.

On reflection Chelsea didn't really cope well after winning the title, and as some of the older players made way for the younger lads coming through the ranks, so the team seemed to lose it's way. Ted was looking to the future I know and some changes had to be made, but not everyone was really up to Jimmy Greaves' standard and the club had an awkward few years of adjustment as they came to terms with what they'd achieved.

Later on at Chelsea I was put in charge of looking after the second team and taking them to away games, and for a while I thought I may become Ted Drake's assistant at some stage but Dave Sexton came in and I left the club. I did apply for the manager's job down at Torquay but didn't get that either, so I made the decision to get out of football even though I thought I had a lot more to offer the game. I then went to the Westminster School where I had sixteen fantastic years working with the children and I have lots of great memories from my time after football.

A couple of years ago I went along to see Jimmy Greaves and Ron Harris performing their stage show in Hoddesdon, Hertfordshire and somebody told them I was in the audience. When they came back on after the interval Jimmy pointed me out to the crowd and thanked me for helping to coach him when he was a youngster - he said some really nice things which I appreciated. Jimmy was always an entertainer, even at sixteen.

Les
Stubbs

I've lived in Wakering, near Southend, all of my life, and apart from my time at Chelsea, plus a brief spell at Bedford Town, all my football has been played within a stone's throw of my village. I played for Barling juniors before progressing through almost every Essex Schoolboy level. My first highlight as a youngster was when our team won the County Championships at Everton's Goodison Park. That was a great occasion and it gave me a taste of what being a professional was like. The earlier you can experience something like that the better, as it opens your eyes and helps you step up a level.

Another factor that helped me aspire to play at a professional level was the fact that my cousin, Peter Samson, had played for Bristol Rovers for about twenty years. I thought if Peter can make the grade, then so can I. My dad had been a good player too until he got wounded during the War, and both my brothers, Den and Ernie, were decent players - so there must have been something in the Stubbs' genes.

When I left school at fourteen I started working as a trainee mechanic at a cycle shop, where I bumped into Southend's Wilf Copping, who was an ex-England international and a fantastic opportunity was offered to me. Wilf had come into the shop to get his bike fixed, but I recognised him and we got talking about football for ages. He seemed really interested in what I was telling him about my team, and me as a player, but I couldn't believe it when, at the end of our chat, he asked me if I'd like to come down to the club for a trial. It seemed like a fairytale, so I jumped at the chance. As soon as I arrived at the ground and saw the team training I knew that all I wanted to be was a footballer, this was better than a 'real' job.

My biggest stroke of luck, though, was having my National Service deferred for six months due to an injured ankle. Because the injury wasn't as bad as they first thought I was able to get fit quickly and resume playing football for Essex - it was in that six month period that Southend United offered me a professional contract. Having 'professional footballer' as your full time occupation when you went in to the Army meant that you had a far easier time. My Commanding Officer and Sergeant Major were both football fanatics, and even though the only match I'd played for Southend when I was called up was for United's second team, the fact that I was a pro was all that mattered. I played for the Southern Command Royal Artillery side which included ex-England International, Harold Hassall.

Around that time I was selected to play for England Youth to help the 1948 Great Britain Olympic side prepare for the games in London, both Jackie French, and myself scored that day, but the match was to prove my only representative game for my country.

I really enjoyed it in the Army and would have probably stayed in the Forces as a full time soldier if it hadn't been for football, but when my National Service was up, I returned to Southend and resumed my football career. My full team debut for United was down at Torquay and I scored two goals, you can't go wrong when that kind of thing happens and it was an incredible day for me personally. The only problem is that the manager and the fans expect the same every week if you get off to a flying start, but at least you have them on your side from day one and the pressure is off to a certain extent. The Southend team was a good one at the time, they had some first class older pros, and for young lads like myself, there was plenty to learn from them. Although I lacked experience, what I did possess was a lot of aerial power and I loved to use my head.

I really established myself at Southend and scored a lot of goals, forty-eight goals in a hundred and eleven games, which isn't a bad record. I was being switched from the left wing to centre-forward, but I must admit that I always preferred to be used as a striker because my left foot wasn't that strong. I felt my strength was making runs into the area and attacking crosses that more skillful players could provide - as I saw a cross about to be whipped in I felt myself grow in height and I loved attacking the near post. I always used to hope that I was lucky enough not to head the ball on the lace side though, if you caught the ball on that side it would sometimes take the skin off your forehead and sting for ages!

Scoring so regularly for Southend got me noticed by bigger sides eventually, which I have to admit was something that frightened the life out of me. Our local paper, the Southend Standard, started running stories almost every week linking me to one club or another and the United manager, Harry Warren, was always quoted saying that the club wanted to hold on to me. I was happy to read that my manager wanted to keep me because it was still early days at the club I thought and I didn't feel prepared to go anywhere else. I'd never even seen a First Division game, let alone considered myself ready to play in one. But within two weeks of Harry Warren telling the local newspaper that I wasn't for sale, I was at Stamford Bridge and felt ten foot tall. I think the offer of £10,000 may have helped change his mind! Believe it or not that was an awful lot of money once.

I didn't have two pennies to rub together, so when the Southend players told me that the only way to make any decent money as a footballer was to move away, the transfer became even more tempting. I had no idea about financial matters and was so naïve. When I asked Ted Drake for a signing on fee he must have realised that too. Ted said to me, "Les, what I'm offering you is the First Division, I'm telling you that you're good enough to make it and when you do I'll do all I can for you." Ted was a man of his word because after I'd broken through and played in the first team for a while, Chelsea paid me about £700 and Ted rounded it up to £1000. But I would have gone to Chelsea for nothing if the truth were known.

Even though I was nervous, the feeling I got when I signed for Chelsea was like walking on air. I remember going up by train to sign and there was thick smog hanging over London. I also vividly recall opening the window and taking deep lung-fulls of air as I approached Leigh-on-Sea. The smogs were dreadful in those days, there was a dirty, brown haze that hung in the air over London and we had to run down The Embankment in it when we were training at Stamford Bridge. Some players even used to wear masks to protect themselves from the fumes as they jogged.

When I first arrived at the club I was so keen during those training runs that I used to sprint flat out up at the front, which used to annoy most of the older players. They would always have a word with me to slow down because the pace I was setting meant they had to work harder. I soon learned to keep them happy. More worrying for me was the quality of Chelsea's junior side, which included the likes of Jimmy Greaves and David Cliss, who were both marvellous players even at that age. They were so good, winning by a hatful of goals every game, that I knew I would always be looking over my shoulder at Chelsea. Imagine how I felt during the Championship season when Seamus O'Connell turned up one week, nobody had ever heard of him, then he scored a hat-trick on his debut. Competition for places was always fierce.

My Blues debut came up at Newcastle, and although Ted had put me down on the team sheet to play at inside-forward, I was pushed up to centre-forward from the start. This suited me down to the ground because their centre-half only came up to my shoulder and I knew there was no way he could out-jump me. I remember how desperate I was not to let anyone down that day.

I didn't have a particularly good start to my Chelsea career to be honest, I struggled for quite some time, only making five appearances that first season and I felt out of sorts. I didn't think my new team mates knew my strengths and it took a little bit of time for them to get to know what kind of player I was - I guess I was in awe of a few of them too. But I knew that as soon as I scored a goal I would start to relax more. At Southend I'd learned that you scored just as many goals mis-kicking the ball as you do from perfect finishing, so as long as a goal came my way, any goal, things would be okay.

March 1955 — Les Stubbs dives in against Blackpool during Chelsea's 0-0 draw

Les Stubbs heads over the Arsenal goalie during a 2-0 Chelsea win

Les Stubbs watches Leicester City's goalie catch the ball

November 1954 — Stubbs involved in a goal-mouth scramble during 2-1 win over Spurs

I was in and out of the team at the start of my second season, 1953-54, then things seemed to click and I became a regular member of the first team. I'd done a lot of talking and a lot of listening, learning from the other players and from the manager which made me more positive in my outlook. For some reason I was troubled by a lot of hamstring pulls in those early days and it was about that time when they cleared up and I was able to get back to full fitness for a decent amount of time.

The feeling of being in the side and part of Chelsea's first team was incredible, so scoring up at Huddersfield just after staking my claim seemed like the icing on the cake. To feel included, being picked on merit and playing well is a feeling that can't be bettered as a footballer. I loved the camaraderie and togetherness and I realised what a great mob that Chelsea team were.

Ted Drake encouraged team bonding as much as he could and enjoyed taking us all away together to build morale. We used to go down to Brighton to play golf, sometimes for a whole week, which the players thought was amazing. Trips like that were so important because, like myself, a fair few players lived away from London and after training would commute back home. So the chance of getting to know each other better socially couldn't do any harm at all. I felt I got on well with everyone, but of all the players, I think I became closest to Peter Brabrook. Even though he was competing for my position, I thought he was a great player, and would go as far as to say that I considered he was better than I was.

There was a lot of local interest in my progress back in Southend, but it's not in my nature for success to go to my head, I would hate it if anyone ever thought I had a big ego. What was so good was that none of my friends treated me any differently and because I still lived where I always had and returned home after training every day, I remained the same old Les in their eyes. I became the warden at the local Youth Centre and organised all the football events and quite a few of them used to travel up to Stamford Bridge on the train with me on match-days to watch me play. My brother-in-law became a Chelsea fanatic and kept a scrapbook for me of all the newspaper cuttings.

The distance involved in commuting to and from Chelsea didn't seem to bother me, the club paid for my season ticket and I used to catch a District Line train from Fenchurch Street to Victoria, where I'd often bump in to Eric 'Pinkie' Parsons and the other Brighton lads who travelled up from the South Coast. Everyone else used to call Eric 'Rabbit', but for a reason I can't explain, he's always been 'Pinky' to me! Nobody else really had nicknames apart from Eric, but most of us had an alternative, 'continental', name that we used to call each other when we wanted to sound a bit more exotic. Leslo Stubbouro I was known as, and if my memory serves me, we used to have knock-about games where everyone would change their names to make them sound more Hungarian or Italian. Don't forget that Hungary had just become the first international side to beat England at Wembley and Puskas and company were probably the best side in the world at that period.

One of my best goals for Chelsea came against Portsmouth at Stamford Bridge in November 1954. I was almost forty-yards out, with the wind behind me and my opponent catching me, I decided to let fly with a ball that weighed almost half a ton. Luck must have been with me that day because it dipped and went in just underneath the bar and Ron Greenwood came running over to me and said, "that's one you will never, ever forget." He was right too! John Harris, our centre-back, told the press after the game that it was one of the best goals he'd ever seen, but I wouldn't go that far, maybe he was winding me up! It was marvellous to score at The Bridge, it's a lovely feeling to see all those fans cheering, especially when the ground was full - the noise was out of this world.

Playing up front with Roy Bentley was a fantastic honour, he was a great player and a great fella. Roy would do anything to help you and he was a good motivator. Sometimes you have to be cruel to be kind when you are the Captain of a great club like Chelsea, but Roy never overstepped the mark, and when you were pulled up by him, you respected what he said and did your best to improve. People often think great captains have to play at the heart of the defence or centre of midfield, but Roy showed that a forward could do just as good a job. Roy certainly knew what he was talking about, and because he was so mobile on the pitch, he was able to drop back and keep players motivated and focussed. My personal view is that Roy was the best player in the team, but it would only be fair to say that I admired everyone in that side and thought they were all far better than me.

The loyalty of the Chelsea fans will never cease to amaze me, groups of supporters even used to travel away on the overseas tours we went on back in the Fifties which was staggering commitment in that era, and to this day I still receive letters from fans. It staggers me that I am still remembered to be honest. I had a pile of postcard-sized photographs, which I would sign and return to any fans that wrote to me, but over the years they've whittled away and the letters became few and far between. But a few weeks ago my first fan's letter for ages dropped through my letter-box and I'm down to my last photo now.

Because Chelsea had never won the First Division before, I didn't get the impression that there was really too much belief that the 1954-55

November 1954 – Parson's cheers Stubbs' cracker during the 3-3 draw at Sunderland

Les Stubbs [second from right] poses for a photo at Jimmy Greaves' wedding

season would be any different. We knew we had a very good side and as the season progressed and we came away with some great results from places like Wolves, Tottenham and Bolton, so the confidence started to grow. When you went to places like Molineux, you knew you were always in for a battle, so to win there we must have had a chance. I scored the winning goal against Wolves that day, what a feeling that was.

That euphoric experience should have been bettered at Fratton Park in our penultimate away game of the season, I scored a perfectly good goal, which should have been the winner and Championship clincher, but the referee disallowed it for some reason or another that I'll never understand. I suppose that shows how fate plays its part, when I think about it now I could have been the player to have settled the title that season. I didn't think about it in those terms at the time though, in fact I'd forgotten about the incident by the time I'd got home!

The celebrations after we'd clinched the title back at The Bridge a week later were marvellous though, seeing the crowd coming onto the pitch to mob the players really was special. I remember we had a dinner with the Board a short while afterwards where the Chairman, Joe Mears, kept standing up and toasting the players one by one. He'd bang his knife on the side of his glass, stand up, call one of our names out, drained his glass, then sit back down again. This went on for quite a while until he couldn't stand up any more, he tried, but he just passed out and smashed his face on the table. I think he may have even broken his nose because I remember seeing the blood spreading out on what had previously been a crisp, white table cloth.

As Champions Chelsea qualified to play in the Charity Shield against the 1955 FA Cup winners, Newcastle United. Unfortunately for me, the venue for the traditional pre-season Cup Final was decided by the flick of a coin and played at the club's home grounds. The following year Wembley became the automatic venue, so I missed my chance of playing below the Twin Towers. It was still a memorable day, Chelsea winning three-nil at Stamford Bridge and I've had the winner's plaque on my mantlepiece to this very day.

The following season was tougher for Chelsea I thought, it was only natural that the teams we were facing raised their games for The Champions, as we always did, it always feels good to have beaten the top dogs, it's always an incentive.

I was broken hearted when I had to leave Chelsea in 1958, but I knew my time was up, Jimmy Greaves had replaced me in the team and when somebody of his class replaces you, you can be pretty sure there's no realistic way back. I was very close to Jimmy, in fact I was a guest at his wedding.

I just had to accept that I'd had a wonderful time at Stamford Bridge, had met some wonderful people and played football with some wonderful colleagues. But I was prepared to adapt to life away from the top flight again, a double deal saw Alan Dicks and myself move back to Southend for £12,500, which was big money for United.

If I'd been able to choose another team to play for it would have been Southend, so at least the fall was a cushioned one to some extent, but things didn't work out as well for me in my second spell. I had a terrible bust up with the club over my wages, I'm not a greedy man, but I had to go on strike because the club had gone back on their word after agreeing to pay me £16 per week.

The club thought they had me over a barrel. They knew that because I was a local lad the chances of moving anywhere else were slim, and I suppose they were right, but I decided to stop playing for them straight away and went to work on a farm while my application for the Fire Brigade was being processed. I remember the Chairman saying to me; "you can't just walk out!", I replied, "you just watch me!"

The ridiculous thing was, by becoming a fireman, my wages dropped to £8 per week, but I had principles and dug my heels in, refusing to play. Then one Friday night the Chairman turned up on my doorstep and offered me the £300 back pay that was required to see me change my mind and turn out for United again.

After Southend I had a year at Bedford Town in 1960, but I decided to hang my boots up as a professional and the Fire Brigade became my second career - although I carried on playing for Wakering until I was fifty-three. I was a physical training officer with the Fire Service for sixteen years and loved every minute of it, it may not have quite compared to running out in front of 75,000 Chelsea fans at the Bridge, but I had some equally happy days.

Seamus
O'Connell

New Year's Day 1955 — O'Connell delivers a cross during Chelsea's 5-2 win at Bolton

March 1955 — Seamus O'Connell scores Chelsea's second in the 2–0 win at Charlton

The son of a wealthy cattle dealer, Seamus was signed from Bishop Auckland, which was the crack amateur side at the time. O'Connell used to commute from Carlisle to play for Chelsea and was often spotted on the train carrying his boots, tied by the laces, round his neck. He made his debut in the infamous six-five defeat to Manchester United, where he scored a hat-trick.

Seamus was virtually a one-season wonder and disappeared to live in Spain after winning his Championship medal - where he has lived ever since. O'Connell's scoring stats during the Championship season prove what an important contribution he made and what an influential short-term signing he was for the club. *Albert Sewell*

Bobby
Smith

Bobby Smith celebrates as Chelsea score up at Blackpool

As a kid, playing for Redcar Boys' Club, I was played at full-back, but before a cup final our striker failed to turn up and I was asked to move up front. That game changed everything for me. I scored four goals that day and it proved to be the start of a journey which would take me on to play fifteen games for England, plus the Championship at Chelsea and the Double with Tottenham Hotspur.

Chelsea had a scout who used to cover my part of Yorkshire, a man called Tom Robinson. He'd watched me twice before having a word with my dad to see if I'd come down to Chelsea and promised my father that if I signed at Stamford Bridge, the club would get him a job away from the pit and into the ICI plant in town. The toxic combination of coal dust and chemicals killed my dad prematurely so football was very much an escape from that life for me. From the age of thirteen I'd been down the mines, working for a year as a blacksmith's mate re-shoeing the pit ponies, it was terrifying and I used to dread going down there. I had to walk for miles underground every day with water and iron stone dropping down all around, I was lucky, football really got me away from all that.

I remember coming down to London to play my first trial game for Chelsea as clear as yesterday. I caught the train from Leeds at seven o'clock early one Thursday morning in 1948, which got into Kings Cross almost eight hours later. I was as nervous as anything, I was only fourteen years old and coming down to London was a huge occasion for me because I had never been outside of Lingdale, the tiny mining village in Yorkshire where I was born.

The club told me that their errand man Charlie would meet me and lo and behold, when I got off the train, I spotted this guy with a sign around his neck saying 'this is Charlie'. He was a lovely fella and he escorted me by taxi to Stamford Bridge where I was introduced to Billy Birrell. I found the manager to be a gentleman and he made me feel at home at Chelsea. I stayed the night with my aunt in London ahead of my trial game against Charlton the next day - I scored three goals and Chelsea won three-one.

But I found London too big, too scary, so I decided to catch the midday train back home the very next day. My dad was really surprised to see me back so soon and said that he'd accompany me back to London and stayed with me for a fortnight which helped me settle in better. He said that I'd always regret it if I didn't give Chelsea my best shot.

Anyway, things did get better for me and I did feel more settled, so I went into digs with two other young players, Andy Bowman and Les Kelly in Britannia Road near Stamford Bridge. We had some great times together in the house, especially when Frank Blunstone joined us. We all had a great laugh together, especially when the playing cards and jugs of scrumpy came out some evenings.

As well as playing for Chelsea's youth side, which was called Tudor Rose, my day-to-day duties mainly consisted of odd jobs around the stadium. I helped clean all the baths and boots ahead of matches at Stamford Bridge, which did me a lot of good at the time. We also swept all the terracing, which had its benefits sometimes, as on more than one occasion myself or one of the other kids would find money on the ground, which we'd share out. One day we found a bag full of half crown coins. When we counted it all out there was over £7 worth, and when you were only paid £5 a week, it was some find!

Because we were kept busy around The Bridge during the day, my training had to take place in the evenings, but we had a very good youth team. Albert Tennant and Dickie Foss were the Tudor Rose coaches and they helped me develop as a striker. One day, after a Chelsea third team match at Leyton Orient, I spotted little Charlie again, he was waiting for me and told me to fetch my boots quickly as the manager had asked him to take me straight to the train to join the first team who were travelling up to Bolton that afternoon. I thought I was just going along for the experience, so when I found out I was playing on the morning of the game, the butterflies started... I was only seventeen. Roy Bentley tried to calm me down, he told me to relax and concentrate on playing my own game, the way I'd been playing to get me selected for the first team squad. Roy has always been a rock for me, he's always been there to look after me. Roy also helped me develop as a player, he used to have special heading exercises which he insisted I did to help me jump higher and become stronger in the air. When he first set up a line of balls on string suspended high in the air, I never thought I'd be able to reach them like he did. He had an amazing ability to hang in the air and still be able to deliver powerful headers. After a while I could reach balls I couldn't have done before and that helped me throughout my career.

I don't remember much about my debut game though, Bolton, who included Nat Lofthouse that day, won one-nil but the game whizzed by. During the rest of that season I played fifteen more League games and five in the F.A. Cup. the following season, on the way to playing Arsenal in the semi-final, we had three cracks at Leeds United in Round Five, finally winning five-one at Villa Park. I scored a hat-trick that day and I remember the great John Charles telling me that he'd had enough of me, "I don't want to bloody see you for weeks and weeks", he said.

When Billy Birrell left at the end of the 1951-52 season I felt quite excited that Ted Drake was coming because of his scoring record, but it was sad to see Billy go because he was such a nice man. My initial hopes soon turned to despair though. After I'd got to know him, I thought Ted Drake was a horrible man. Ted made it clear he didn't like me and I never really got a chance at Chelsea with him as manager.

My troubles all stemmed from an incident in training one day, we were playing a practice match and myself and Ken Armstrong went in for a challenge. We collided awkwardly and Ken ended up breaking his arm. There was nothing nasty about it, but Ted had a right go at me. When you're a young kid and the manager is bawling at you, you don't know what to say, but I told him I didn't mean to hurt anyone. Roy Bentley really came to my defence, he was the only player in a position to stand up to Drake. He asked Ted what he expected me to have done going in for a fifty-fifty challenge like that? Then Roy told me to walk away. Ted said something as I left, then I heard Roy tell him off because he didn't think it was right that the manager was blaming me for something unavoidable - even Armstrong admitted it wasn't my fault. But from that day Ted Drake made it all too clear that he didn't like me. I was happy to fight for my place though.

In the build up to the Championship Ted brought in so many strikers, so apart from Roy Bentley, none of the centre forwards had an extended run in the team. Along with myself, Les Stubbs and Seamus O'Connell, we were all swapped about as the manager tried to find what he thought was Chelsea's most effective forward line. Although it gave me the needle at times, I knew that all I could do was carry on scoring in the reserves and stake my claim, which I did. In fact I was scoring at such a rate that it must have been getting quite embarrassing for Drake when he didn't pick me. What really baffled me was even though I didn't score myself that season, whenever I played, Chelsea were a very dangerous outfit. The combination of Roy Bentley and myself coincided with a purple patch - we won three-one at Newcastle and drew three-all at home to West Brom. A big plus point was that even though the competition for a first team place was fierce, it didn't affect the atmosphere or relationships between the players and we still all get on well today, all these years later.

Peter Brabrook was another forward on the fringes of the first team at the time, who went on to make a big name for himself at Stamford Bridge after I left for Spurs. Along with Peter Sillett, the three of us were part of the England World Cup squad who travelled to Sweden. It was a shame that I didn't get the chance to play during the tournament, Tom Finney tried his hardest to get me selected but the selectors voted three to two to stick with Derek Kevan. But it was a tremendous experience to travel to the tournament. When I got picked to go I was in two heavens, not just one.

1951 — Exeter's goalie Singleton and Bobby Smith race for the ball during a Cup replay

But even improving as a player didn't seem to sway Drake's opinion of me and after training one day I was told that he wanted to see me in his office. He told me that Bill Nicholson at Spurs wanted to sign me because of the goals I had been scoring in the reserves. Drake told me that I should go because there was "no future at Stamford Bridge" for me, but even when he outlined his feelings so bluntly, I still told him I wanted to stay at Chelsea. I had come down as a young kid and had grown up around Stamford Bridge, so I was against the move. Despite my problem with the manager, I really cared about Chelsea. But when I went back downstairs and told Roy Bentley he told me I was mad, he said he would have jumped at the chance in my position and underlined the fact that with Ted Drake at Chelsea I was never going to be given the opportunity to prove myself. Roy recommended that I should agree to a move before Spurs changed their minds. Luckily I caught up with Drake as he was just about to get into his car, so I quickly walked over and told him that I'd changed my mind about being transferred to White Hart Lane. So, eight months after Chelsea won the title, I became a Spurs player.

It's funny how things work out because I'd scored against Tottenham just before I signed and had absolutely no idea that a couple of weeks later I'd be a Spurs player myself. The goal I scored that day was a bit fortunate I've got to admit, a cross was fired in from the wing which hit my toe and flew into the top corner of the goal. I remember the Spurs 'keeper, Ted Ditchburn, calling me a "lucky bastard" as the ball hit the back of the net and when I met up with him for my first training session at White Hart Lane, we had a laugh about the goal. I had an angry showdown with Ted Drake before I left where I told him that it was my intention to make him regret getting rid of me and I would ram all the spiteful things he had done to me down his throat.

A manager has the power to make you or break you. Whether Drake got the needle with me because I was a similar type of player to how he was at Arsenal I don't know, maybe he thought there was some sort of competition between the two of us. Bill Nicholson was a completely different man altogether. But maybe, just maybe, my troubles at Chelsea helped me become a hungrier, more determined and focussed player for the rest of my career.

I was never a big headed player, I know that at Spurs I was lucky to have players around me to achieve what I'd missed out on six years earlier. But I would have loved to have still been at Chelsea and helped them achieve the Double like I did at Tottenham - if I could have achieved just one thing in football, I would have chosen for it to have happened at Stamford Bridge. Chelsea were struggling when Spurs

1951 — [L–R] James Smith, Jimmy D'Arcey, Bobby Smith & Roy Bentley during training

started to do well and I am sure Blues fans were looking across London and asking why Jimmy Greaves and myself had been sold. I felt sorry for Chelsea that Drake got rid of me, I think it would have been far better for Chelsea in the long run if I'd stayed at Stamford Bridge.

My time at Chelsea certainly helped me gain a more physical presence on the pitch because after moving to North London I had the reputation of being a hard man at White Hart Lane. Dave Mackay had a similar tag at Spurs, but it was only the two of us who were seen in that light, the rest of that team were a bunch of fairies!

I remember travelling away to Europe with Spurs where Jimmy Greaves was really singled out and kicked all over the place, one tackle was so bad that his boot came off. Dave Mackay and myself had a word with each other and decided to sort the defender responsible out. At the next corner Dave hit him from one side and I caught him right in the gut from the other. Jimmy was still so wound up that he went running over and shouted at the crumpled player, "that serves you bloody well right!" With that the referee sent Jimmy off as he was on the scene so quickly afterwards that the official thought he'd decked the defender.

I would never normally go around lumping people though, but I made sure I never ever backed out of a challenge and put my all into the game. I was the same for England, I knew if I pulled out of a tackle, or backed off when jumping up with the goalie, I was the one who would get hurt. This did see me have a few bust-ups, and I'll never forget Glasgow Rangers' Eric Caldow's father coming onto me after a Scotland - England game where I broke his son's leg. He accused me of everything under the sun and was threatening to get me for what I'd done, so I told him if Caldow hadn't have backed out he wouldn't have got hurt, then I went to walk away. With that the dad came for me, but the guy I was with stepped in and gave him the biggest smack in the face I've ever seen.

I am glad to have played in the era I did, I find most of the football I watch these days so boring. Apart from a handful of obvious exceptions the skill has been taken away and the amount of foreign players has become ridiculous. I really feel for the young English players who are trying to make the grade these days. Even though I didn't have things all my own way, there was still a chance for me to move to another top flight club and fight for a place in the England team. That just doesn't seem to be the case any more and I am sure English football will pay the price in the long run.

Special
Mentions

Billy Birrell

Billy is often overlooked when Chelsea's Championship is mentioned, but he should take a lot of credit for having the vision to start the club's youth scheme. Billy sensed that a youth team could nurture a lot of homegrown talent over the years. The team was called Tudor Rose and they played on a pitch at The Welsh Harp over at Hendon, a real wind-swept, rough and ready ground that helped turn the boys into men. Birrell also deserves a lot of credit for securing a lot of the signings that Ted Drake depended upon to build a Championship winning squad. *Albert Sewell*

Joe Mears

Joe was the Chairman of Chelsea when they won the title and later became the Chairman of the Football Association. Joe was a real Chelsea fan, but he sadly died in Norway on the eve of the 1966 World Cup. England were playing a friendly in Oslo and one morning after breakfast he dropped dead while walking in a park. Joe was the father of Brian, who was a more recent Chairman at Stamford Bridge.

Albert Sewell

John Battersby

Following Billy Birrell's resignation in 1952, John was promoted from assistant-secretary to secretary. It allowed Ted Drake a lot more time to concentrate on team matters. 'JB', as he became known by most people at Chelsea, was with the club around thirty years. It was a sad day when he resigned to move down to Devon to run a post office. What a contrast from London life! Now in his eighties, he lives in Wales. We keep in touch. *Albert Sewell*

Chelsea Legends Club

The Chelsea Legends Club was founded in 1997 by Chelsea enthusiast Katie Cheeseman. Initially the club was formed to assist past Chelsea players to attend games. The Chelsea Legends Club would buy tickets from the funds raised by its members thus enabling the ex players to attend games at Stamford Bridge.

Today the club represents the interests of many ex-Chelsea players including former Blues Captain and patron Ron 'Chopper' Harris, along with many members of the 1955 Championship team. Katie arranges everything from small private dinners to public autograph signings on behalf of the boys.

The club also has a very active supporters club with an extensive UK membership and Katie's enthusiasm is reflected in the wide range of events and football trips arranged throughout the season. The club also travel to Europe and to many away fixtures, as well as running both youth and adult coaching courses where fans can learn first hand from the likes of Ron Harris and Tommy Baldwin who are regular coaches with the scheme. Katie Cheeseman can be contacted at the Chelsea Legends Club, 19 Dredges Close, Bramley, GU5 0AA.

1954-55
Statistics

1954-55 League Table

		Pld	Home					Away						Overall						Pts	GA
			W	D	L	F	A	W	D	L	F	A	W	D	L	F	A		
1	Chelsea	42	11	5	5	43	29	9	7	5	38	28	20	12	10	81	57	52	1.42
2	Wolves	42	13	5	3	58	30	6	5	10	31	40	19	10	13	89	70	48	1.27
3	Portsmouth	42	13	5	3	44	21	5	7	9	30	41	18	12	12	74	62	48	1.19
4	Sunderland	42	8	11	2	39	27	7	7	7	25	27	15	18	9	64	54	48	1.19
5	Man United	42	12	4	5	44	30	8	3	10	40	44	20	7	15	84	74	47	1.14
6	Aston Villa	42	11	3	7	38	31	9	4	8	34	42	20	7	15	72	73	47	0.99
7	Man City	42	11	5	5	45	36	7	5	9	31	33	18	10	14	76	69	46	1.10
8	Newcastle	42	12	5	4	53	27	5	4	12	36	50	17	9	16	89	77	43	1.16
9	Arsenal	42	12	3	6	44	25	5	6	10	25	38	17	9	16	69	63	43	1.10
10	Burnley	42	11	3	7	29	19	6	6	9	22	29	17	9	16	51	48	43	1.06
11	Everton	42	9	6	6	32	24	7	4	10	30	44	16	10	16	62	68	42	0.91
12	Huddersf'd	42	10	4	7	28	23	4	9	8	35	45	14	13	15	63	68	41	0.93
13	Sheff Utd	42	10	3	8	41	34	7	4	10	29	52	17	7	18	70	86	41	0.81
14	Preston	42	8	5	8	47	33	8	3	10	36	31	16	8	18	83	64	40	1.30
15	Charlton	42	8	6	7	43	34	7	4	10	33	41	15	10	17	76	75	40	1.01
16	Tottenham	42	9	4	8	42	35	7	4	10	30	38	16	8	18	72	73	40	0.99
17	West Brom	42	11	5	5	44	33	5	3	13	32	63	16	8	18	76	96	40	0.79
18	Bolton	42	11	6	4	45	29	2	7	12	17	40	13	13	16	62	69	39	0.90
19	Blackpool	42	8	6	7	33	26	6	4	11	27	38	14	10	18	60	64	38	0.94
20	Cardiff City	42	9	4	8	41	38	4	7	10	21	38	13	11	18	62	76	37	0.82
21	Leicester	42	9	6	6	43	32	3	5	13	31	54	12	11	19	74	86	35	0.86
22	Sheff Wed	42	7	7	7	42	38	1	3	17	21	62	8	10	24	63	100	26	0.63

1954-55 Appearances & Goals

	LEAGUE		CUP	
	App	Goals	App	Goals
Parsons	42	11	3	1
Saunders	42	1	3	0
Bentley	41	21	3	0
McNichol	40	14	2	1
Armstrong	39	1	3	0
Willemse	36	1	3	0
Harris	31	0	0	0
Stubbs	27	5	3	1
Robertson	26	0	1	0
Blunstone	23	3	3	1
Greenwood	21	0	0	0
Sillett	21	6	3	0
Wicks	21	1	3	0
Lewis	17	6	0	0
Thomson	16	0	0	0
O'Connell	10	7	1	1
Smith	4	0	0	0
Brabrook	3	0	0	0
Dicks	1	0	0	0
Edwards	1	0	0	0
Own Goals	4			